Cine Photography Made Easy

When friends ask the dreaded question, 'Would you like to see our holiday films?' do you groan inwardly, force a smile and say 'Yes, we'd love to'? Home movies need not be like that. They should instead be something to look forward to, enjoyed by everyone. This book tells you how to make films like that with essentially simple equipment, and how to present them with a professional touch. It is written for the beginner and deals only with Super 8 cine photography, since this is the type of camera that is now used almost exclusively by amateur cine photographers.

Widen Your Horizons with this series

Remember that we cater for all interests. See for yourself with our expanding list of titles.

Places to see

Scottish Islands – Tom Weir
Dartmoor – Crispin Gill

Leisure activities

Good Photography Made Easy – Derek Watkins
Looking at Churches – David Bowen
Pony Trekking – Edward Hart
Railways for Pleasure – Geoffrey Body
Sea Fishing for Fun – Alan Wrangles

Sporting

The Art of Good Shooting – J. E. M. Ruffer
Archery for All – Daniel Roberts
Rowing for Everyone – Christopher Chant

Forthcoming titles

Wine Making
Dinghy Sailing

Cine Photography Made Easy

Derek Watkins

David & Charles
Newton Abbot London
North Pomfret (VT) Vancouver

ISBN 0 7153 7437 0
Library of Congress Catalog Card Number 77–74354

Photoset in 11 on 13 Bembo
and printed and bound in Great Britain
by Redwood Burn Limited, Trowbridge & Esher
for David & Charles (Publishers) Limited
Brunel House   Newton Abbot   Devon

Published in the United States of America
by David & Charles Inc
North Pomfret   Vermont 05053   USA

Published in Canada
by Douglas David & Charles Limited
1875 Welch Street   North Vancouver   BC

Contents

1 How cine photography works

In basic terms, a cine camera is just like any other camera, the essential difference being the speed or frequency with which it takes photographs. With a still camera you compose your picture, press the shutter release, and wind on the film manually ready for the next shot, while with a cine camera the film is exposed and wound on in rapid sequence all the time you hold your finger on the shutter release button. In fact the cine camera takes pictures at the rate of eighteen every second, each picture being slightly different from the one before it. When you project these photographs they are fed through the projector at the same rate – eighteen pictures a second – and because this speed is too fast for the human eye to see each picture as a single still photograph the whole sequence appears as a moving picture.

A cine or movie camera consists basically of a light-tight casing with a lens at one end which takes the light reflected from your subject and focuses it to form an image on the film which is at the other end of the casing. On simple cameras the lens is usually of fixed focus and is pre-set when the camera is manufactured, to a point which enables all objects to be sharply recorded from a relatively close distance right to infinity. More expensive cameras often have lenses which can be adjusted so that objects at different distances from the camera can be focused accurately on the film, and some cameras are fitted with zoom lenses which allow you to alter the size of your subject within the picture area. Within the lens, or sometimes behind it, is a device called the diaphragm or aperture which adjusts the diameter of the lens and so controls the amount of light entering the camera and reaching the film. On simple cine cameras you have to set the aperture yourself after referring to exposure tables or an exposure meter, but on an increasing number of modern cameras the aperture is controlled automatically according to the light conditions. Behind the lens is a shutter which controls the amount of time that light emerging from the lens actually falls on the film. Normally, of course, the shutter is closed but as soon as you press the shutter release button the shutter opens to expose the film. Only the more advanced and expensive cine cameras have more than one shutter speed; most amateur cameras have a single shutter speed of around 1/30th second. This means that all adjustments for varying light conditions must be carried out with the aperture control.

Since movies depend for their effect on the camera taking one picture after another very rapidly, the camera has to have some mechanical means of winding on the film after each single exposure and positioning the next frame accurately behind the lens. This job is done by a motor – usually electric these days – which drives a claw. The claw engages the small perforations down one edge of the film and advances it exactly the same amount each time. In addition to driving the claw, the motor also operates the shutter and the take-up mechanism for the exposed film. Power for the motor is supplied by small batteries which are usually placed in the camera's handgrip.

In automatic cine cameras the aperture setting is controlled by a system of electronic and mechanical devices which sense the brightness of the light reflected from the subject and adjust the size of the aperture to the correct setting. The sensing device is called a photo-conducting cell and is positioned either alongside the lens or, in reflex cameras, behind the lens.

Film for Super 8 cameras comes in a cartridge which you simply slot into the camera; there is no threading of film or other fiddling about involved. On the front corner of the cartridge is a small notch, the position of which indicates the speed or sensitivity of the film in the cartridge. This notch engages a lever on automatic cameras which adjusts the control system to compensate for the film speed, so that your film will be correctly exposed.

Each sequence you film is controlled by a shutter release button or lever which is generally built into the camera's handgrip or sometimes the top or front of the camera. When you operate this button the motor in the camera starts to turn, advancing the film frame by frame and exposing it. The camera will continue to take pictures until you remove your finger from the release button. In addition to the normal release button operated by your finger, some cameras have a socket for a cable release. This is extremely useful when you are using your camera on a tripod as it allows you to film without actually touching the camera, and so removes the danger of jarring it. A second cable release socket is often

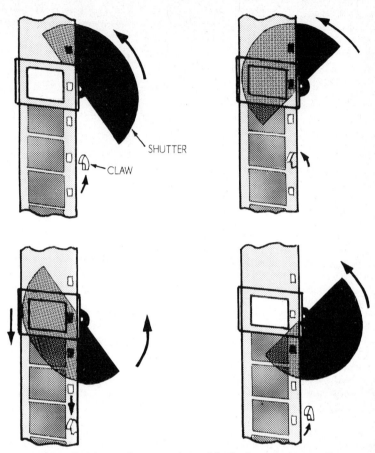

How the shutter and claw mechanism work-*Top left*: The shutter is open exposing a frame
Top right: As the shutter closes the claw engages a perforation in the film
Bottom left: While the shutter remains closed the claw pulls the film down
Bottom right: The shutter opens to expose the next frame as the claw disengages

included which enables the camera to take just one picture at a time; this is particularly useful for time lapse photography which I shall deal with later in the book.

So that you can sight and compose your films accurately, every cine camera has some sort of viewfinder. This may be anything from a simple optical device which produces a small image of the subject, to a reflex viewing system which enables you to see your subject through the camera lens. For simple cameras the frame type of viewfinder is entirely adequate, but for more advanced cameras which may have a zoom lens or a focusing system, the reflex viewfinder system is very much to be preferred. Generally speaking, what you see through the reflex viewfinder is exactly what you will see on the screen when your film is projected. Another problem which the reflex viewfinder solves is that of parallax. Because a normal optical viewfinder and the camera lens are physically separated by a few inches, they see the subject from slightly different viewpoints and this difference is called parallax. When you are filming from a reasonably large distance from the subject parallax is so small as to be insignificant, but when the filming distance is down to about five feet or so, it can cause heads to be chopped off or unwanted objects appearing at the edge of the picture. Because the reflex viewfinder allows you to look through the lens of the camera, parallax is eliminated. Some optical viewfinders have a pair of small marks, one at either side of the main frame, to indicate the effective top or side of the frame for close range filming.

Many of the more expensive movie cameras, especially those which have fully controllable exposure, have an indicator in the viewfinder window to enable you to adjust the aperture correctly while filming. This usually takes the form of a needle or pointer which moves as you alter the aperture control, and the idea is to align this needle with a fixed pointer. Automatic cameras usually have some form of indicator which tells you when there is insufficient light for successful filming, and some also have an indicator which tells you when the light is too bright and will give over-exposure.

Filming Speed

The standard rate at which a Super 8 cine camera films is 18 frames per second (fps) and the standard speed at which the projector shows the film is also 18 fps; it has to be to give a realistic speed of movement on the screen. If you shoot film in the camera at a higher speed than 18 fps, the film will obviously pass through the camera more quickly. Say, for example, that you shoot at 36 fps instead of the usual 18, you will use twice as much film as you normally would, but when you show this piece of film the projector will pass it through at the standard 18 fps and this means that it will take twice as long to pass through the projector as it did through the camera. The net result is that the action on the screen will appear to take place in slow motion: at half the normal speed, in fact.

Now if you go the other way and shoot film at a slower speed than 18 fps, the result will be speeded-up action when you show the film at the standard 18 fps in your projector. So film shot at, say, 9 fps will produce action on the screen at twice the normal speed.

Most movie cameras in the cheaper price range are fitted with only a single filming speed – the standard 18 fps – but many projectors have two or more speeds, so you can still achieve slow motion or speeded-up action even if your camera is only a simple one. To be fair, though, the results are never as good when you control the speed with the projector.

Choosing a Cine Camera

Movie cameras range in complexity and price from very simple basic models at around £30–£50 up to highly advanced cameras incorporating all kinds of special features and costing upwards of £500. So the particular model you buy will be influenced by two factors: what you want to do with the camera, and the size of your budget.

Assuming that you want to use your camera just to make records of your summer holidays, the family at Christmas, and other similar occasions, and do not see yourself getting involved in more advanced film making, an inexpensive, simple movie camera will be perfectly adequate for your needs. Indeed, if you buy a more complex camera, costing maybe three or four times as much, you may well find that you never use many of the features and have therefore wasted your money. Or the advanced features may tend to intimidate you and put you off using your camera, which is even worse.

Simple movie cameras – Kodak XL330 and XL360

The one feature I would strongly urge you to look for when buying your cine camera is a zoom lens. Movies shot entirely with a lens of fixed focal length can become rather boring unless you make use of gimmicky camera angles and other devices. But a zoom lens allows you not only to close in on your subject (or open out from it) without actually moving, it also enables you to choose the most appropriate viewpoint and perspective for non-zoom shots. Cameras with this type of lens start in price at around £60.

Another feature worth looking for is a manual over-ride device on the automatic exposure control fitted to most cameras, even the cheapest. There are times, as I shall explain later, when the automatic exposure system will give over or under exposure of your main subject because of the way it measures light. On these occasions it is as well to know that you can compensate by simply operating a lever on your camera.

However, if you are interested in becoming more involved with cine photography as a major hobby and you want to progress eventually to making more advanced films, you would probably do better to buy a technically more complex camera. Maybe you want to be able to handle slow motion and speeded action filming, so you would need a camera with several filming speeds. Or perhaps you would like to produce time-lapse sequences – of a flower opening, for example – so a single frame exposure feature would be something to look for when you choose your camera. These more advanced cameras start in price at around £100 and increase according to the number of additional features. But you should

A more complex cine camera – Minolta Autopak – 8 D12

be able to buy one which will do just about everything you would want, for a maximum of about £200. Above this figure you begin to get into the professional Super 8 class in which the increase in price is brought about mainly by increasing toughness and perhaps the addition of a feature or two which the amateur would use only very infrequently. So the

Top class professional standard camera Eumig 830XL

decision you have to make, then, is whether you want to spend one or two hundred pounds more for a little extra in the way of facilities.

Film for Your Camera

All film for Super 8 movie cameras is supplied in easy-to-load cartridges. No other type of 8mm movie film will fit a Super 8 camera. Recently introduced Super 8 sound cameras (which I shall deal with in a later chapter) take special cartridges of sound film. These cameras will also accept normal silent Super 8 film if you want to make silent movies, but silent cameras will not take the sound film cartridges since they are about half an inch deeper than the silent film cartridge.

When Super 8 was introduced in 1965 as an alternative, easier to use system for the amateur, one of the main advantages it was said to offer was increased image size on the film over the old Standard 8 system, which was at that time the standard amateur film size. While the old Standard 8 frame size was 0·192 × 0·145in, the Super 8 frame is 0·224 × 0·116in, some thirty-five per cent bigger. And because Super 8 projectors use a larger proportion of the image than Standard 8, there is a further increase in usable image size up to a total of fifty per cent. The net result of this is a significantly sharper, better quality picture on the screen.

Another big advantage that Super 8 has is its easy-loading facility. All you have to do is open the camera, drop in the film cartridge, close the camera, and press the shutter release; a far cry from the old Standard 8 system where you had to thread the film manually round pressure pads, through the gate, and on to the take-up spool. This could often take minutes to carry out instead of the few seconds it takes to load a Super 8 camera.

A Super 8 cartridge contains fifty feet of film ready loaded and threaded; the whole system is fool-proof and pretty well jam-proof, too. The film and its associated mechanism is loaded into a sealed plastic casing with a built-in pressure pad to keep the film correctly aligned in the camera gate. In the front of the cartridge, at the opposite side to the film aperture, is a series of notches which automatically set various functions when you insert the cartridge into the camera. The top notch sets the camera's meter to the correct speed for the film in the cartridge. The next one down is a locating slit to ensure that the cartridge is correctly positioned within the camera. And at the bottom is a third notch which controls the filter built into practically all Super 8 cameras, behind the lens. The reason for this filter is to enable Super 8 colour film – which is usually designed for use in artificial light – to be used also in daylight. The filter is normally operated manually by sliding a small lever, but on some cameras, attaching movie lights for filming indoors automatically moves the filter out of the light path. Some cameras also have a small lever which operates the filter and which protrudes into the film chamber in the position where the bottom notch on the film cartridge is located.

There are a few films now available which are designed for use

Super 8 cartridges. Note the top notch, the size of which depends on the speed of the film and sets the automatic exposure mechanism in the camera. The film on the left is 40 ASA; that on the right 160 ASA

in daylight. These films are loaded into cartridges which do not have the bottom notch. When you place the cartridge in the camera, therefore, the front of the cartridge presses the filter lever and automatically removes the filter from behind the lens.

Colour films

Practically all the Super 8 film used for home movies is colour film, for the simple reason that most people prefer realistic colour pictures to black and white. As I have already pointed out, most Super 8 colour film is balanced for artificial light (it is known as Type A film) and is used in daylight by placing the built-in conversion filter in the light path behind the camera lens. If your camera is one of the very few that have no built-

Most cine cameras have a switch or lever to operate the built-in filter. Make sure it is set to the type of light you are filming in

in filter – some early Super 8 cameras were not so fitted – you will need to buy one. The correct type is the Kodak Wratten No 85 or its equivalent which you can buy from any good photographic dealer.

The reason for standardising on artificial light film for universal use is simple. When you use any colour film in conjunction with a conversion filter, the filter absorbs some of the light and gives, in effect, a loss of film speed. Now because daylight is invariably much brighter than artificial light you need maximum film speed when filming in artificial light. The No 85 conversion filter cuts the effective film speed by slightly less than half – not too great a loss – so you can use the artificial light type film in both forms of lighting without too many problems. On the other hand, if the camera manufacturers had standardised on daylight film to be used in conjunction with a filter for filming in artificial light, they would have been faced with much bigger problems. For a start, the filter for converting daylight film for use in artificial light cuts the effective film speed to a quarter of its normal value, so you would have, in effect, a comparatively fast film for daylight use but an impractically slow one for indoor filming. And the quality of colour is generally better with arti-ficial light film converted for daylight than with daylight film converted for use in artificial light.

The speed of a film is expressed as a figure followed by the initials ASA or DIN. These are the initials of the American and German standards authorities. There is also a British authority denoted by the initials BSI; its standards for film speeds are identical with the American standard and the initials are rarely used. Most colour films for Super 8 users are fairly slow in speed – around 40 ASA in artificial light – which means effec-tively 25 ASA in daylight. These films are entirely adequate for most purposes, since movie cameras tend to have fairly large aperture lenses which enable you to film successfully in practically any lighting con-ditions. However, a few years ago, Kodak introduced a high speed movie colour film – Ektachrome 160 Type A – which has meant that you can now make movies in really dim lighting such as ordinary dom-estic lighting, outdoors at night, and in really subdued conditions. Kodak have also introduced a special version of Ektachrome 160 called Type G which has the very unusual property of being usable in any type of lighting – daylight, tungsten artificial lighting, fluorescent lighting, even candle light – *without any kind of filter*. This makes the film particu-larly suitable for mixed lighting situations; in other words, scenes indoors which are lit partly by daylight and partly by artificial light. Normal colour films will not cope satisfactorily with such situations. If you use the film with a daylight conversion filter the parts of the scene lit by artificial light will have a reddish cast but if you use the film without the filter the daylight illuminated areas will have a blue cast.

Colour films are usually sold with processing rights, that is to say you pay for the processing with the price of the film and simply post the film back to the manufacturer for processing when you have shot it. But both versions of Kodak's Ektachrome 160 are sold *without* processing rights so you can send the film to any processing laboratory you like, or, if you have the facilities and the enthusiasm, you can process it yourself.

Black and white film

While most home movies these days are shot on colour film, black and white movies have a certain appeal of their own, and in some cases where

For low light situations use a high speed film such as Ektachrome 160

colour is not of fundamental importance to the subject, black and white can produce a film with more impact and interest than colour. Unfortunately, the number of black and white films in Super 8 size has diminished in recent years, but Kodak again have a suitable material in their Tri-X, which is a high speed film suitable for use in both daylight and artificial light without the need for a filter. The cartridge in which the film is loaded has no filter notch, so the filter for colour film is automatically removed from the light path when you put the cartridge in the camera.

Which film?

From the films which are available to you in Super 8 cartridges, you will find that the normal slow speed colour film, such as Kodachrome 40 or Agfachrome, will be perfectly suitable for most of your filming – holiday films shot during normal daylight, weddings, Christmas movies indoors, and other special occasions. This type of film has a fine grain structure, produces very sharp pictures, and gives bright, saturated colours.

If you want to shoot film in the late evening or in normal domestic lighting conditions, choose a high speed colour film such as Kodak Ektachrome 160 Type A or, if there is likely to be more than one type of lighting, Type G.

And finally, if you want to make a documentary type of film, or perhaps film a do-it-yourself project – situations where colour is not too important – to create added drama, use black and white film.

2 Handling your cine camera

When you have bought your cine camera, no matter how simple or how complex, you must learn how to get the most out of it. All movie cameras have certain limitations, even the very advanced and expensive models, and what you must do is find out what these limitations are and learn to use the camera within them. But first you must learn the basic fundamentals of camera handling: loading the camera, focusing on your subject, setting the correct exposure, and shooting the film. The best way to start to do this is by reading the instruction booklet that comes with your camera. I know that sounds like stating the obvious, but it is surprising how strong the temptation is to play with the camera first and read *how* you should handle it later. So read your instruction booklet carefully from cover to cover, then go through it again with the camera in front of you, operating each control as you come to it in the booklet. This is by far the best and quickest way to familiarise yourself with the basic operations of the camera and to ensure that when you put a film into it you will be able to produce a technically successful film straight away.

The instruction booklet supplied with your camera is the most important piece of literature you can read about that camera because it deals specifically with your particular model. Anything else that you read on the subject can only give general information, so please treat this chapter as supplementary to the information in the instruction booklet.

Loading Your Super 8

Nothing could be simpler than loading a Super 8 movie camera with film. The whole system has been designed so that even the complete beginner cannot possibly load the camera incorrectly. All you have to do is open the back or side of the camera, drop in the pre-loaded, pre-threaded film cartridge, close the camera, and you are ready to shoot. The film cartridge will only fit into the camera correctly one way round and all the meter and motor couplings inside the camera engage automatically when you insert the cartridge. The whole system really is fool proof.

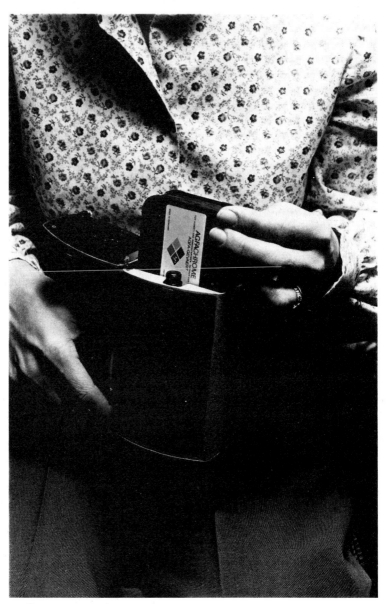

Loading a conventional cine camera

When the whole fifty-foot length of film has been exposed in the camera, the cartridge is just as easy to remove as it was to load. Then you simply put it into a special envelope packed with the film, address it to the processing laboratory and pop it into the nearest post box. A week or so later your film will come back to you on a spool ready for projection. Incidentally, if you have a cartridge of film which you have removed from its sealed foil packing at some time earlier, you can easily tell whether it has been exposed in the camera or not; if it has been exposed, a short length of film visible in the opening at the front of the cartridge will have small notches cut into each side and the word EXPOSED printed on the surface of the film. An unexposed film has no notches and, of course, the word EXPOSED is not printed on it.

When a film has passed through the camera the word EXPOSED appears on the film in the film aperture

Since the film is sealed inside its cartridge, you can load and unload your movie camera in any kind of lighting conditions, but I think it is

a

Depth of field depends on the lens aperture and this, in turn, depends on the brightness of the light. In dull weather, depth of field is shallow so you can have either close subjects (a) in focus OR distant subjects (b). In brighter conditions both subjects are sharply in focus (c)

b

c

advisable to avoid letting direct bright sunlight fall on the front opening
of the cartridge where the film is visible. Instead, try to load the film in
the shade or turn your back to the sun and load in the shadow of your
own body.

Focusing

If yours is a simple movie camera, you will not need to worry about focusing because the chances are that your camera will have a fixed focus
lens. What this means is simply that the lens is set by the manufacturer in
a position that will produce sharp pictures at any distance from a few feet
to infinity. This depth of field, as it is called, or zone of sharpness depends
on two factors: the actual distance of the lens from the film in the camera
and the working aperture of the lens. Now the working aperture
depends in turn on the brightness of the light you are filming by. In
bright sunshine the aperture will be fairly small, while in dull conditions
it will be considerably larger to let more light into the camera to fall on
the film.

Depth of field is greatest at small apertures and least at larger apertures
so you will be able to film closer to your subject in bright sunshine than
in dull weather.

You will often be able to find the effective zone of sharpness for various lighting conditions given in the instruction manual with the camera. If it is not shown there, you should be able to get the information by writing to the manufacturer of the camera. A table showing the depth of field for typical lenses is included in the Appendices at the end of this book.

If your camera is the type with a variable focus lens you must set the focus control for each picture sequence you shoot. With fairly simple movie cameras you have to estimate the distance of your subject or, if you want to be really accurate, measure it with a tape measure, then transfer the distance to the focusing scale on your camera. Some simple cameras make this somewhat easier by having distance symbols as well as actual distances in feet or metres engraved on the scale. For example, there may be a symbol showing two or three human figures; if you are filming a group of people at about fifteen feet distance from the camera, this is the symbol you would set your lens to. More advanced movie cameras, however, have what is known as a reflex viewfinding system. This means that when you look through the viewfinder of the camera you are actually looking through the taking lens. This means that, not only can you see exactly what picture area is recorded on the film, but also you can see just when your subject is sharply focused. So using one of these cameras is simply a matter of adjusting the focusing control until the image in the viewfinder appears sharp. A few cameras have an auxiliary rangefinder device in the centre of the view-finder image. These usually take the form of a split area in which a pair of images come together when the camera is accurately focused, to form a single superimposed image.

Focusing the camera is achieved by simply turning the lens mount which is marked with distances in feet or metres, or both, and may sometimes, as I have already pointed out, have distance symbols. You simply set the appropriate distance figure or symbol against a reference mark on the fixed part of the lens mount and the camera is focused. What you are in fact doing is varying the distance between the lens and the film so that any object at any distance from the camera above a few feet can be accurately focused upon. The further you move the lens from the film plane, the closer is the distance focused. As with simple cameras, the amount of your picture that will be sharply focused will depend on the aperture at which you use the lens.

Exposure

Virtually every Super 8 cine camera available on the market at present is fully automatic from the exposure point of view and this frees you from what is to many people the most complicated part of filming – getting the exposure right. All you do, in fact, is simply point the camera at your subject, press the shutter release button or switch, and the aperture is automatically adjusted to the correct size to suit the lighting conditions. The shutter speed, of course, is fixed because it is controlled by the filming speed; with cameras which have more than one speed, the aperture is automatically changed when you alter the filming speed to compensate for the effectively faster or slower shutter speed. And with Super 8 cameras, as I have already mentioned, you do not even have to set the correct film speed on the camera; this is done automatically when you insert the film cartridge into the camera. One point to beware of though, if you want to use a high speed film such as Kodak Ektachrome 160, is to check with the instruction book supplied with your camera to see that the range of the automatic exposure control extends as far as the speed of this film – 160 ASA. Some early Super 8 cameras have automatic exposure systems which do not extend this far and if you try to use a high speed film with one of these cameras the resulting shots will be ruined by over-exposure.

Automatic exposure control will give correctly exposed pictures in the majority of cases and most cameras incorporate some sort of indicator which appears in the viewfinder when there is insufficient light to film by. However, there are occasions when automatic exposure control does not give the best possible results and many movie cameras incorporate some sort of manual over-ride which enables you to alter the automatic exposure control slightly. Cases when this manual over-ride is extremely useful are when the subject you are filming is either predominantly dark or predominantly light. The reason for this is that exposure meters such as those built into Super 8 cine cameras, take an average value of all the tones in any particular scene and see them as a single mid tone. The meter then sets the lens aperture in the camera to give an exposure for this average. In the case of a predominantly dark subject, most of the tones reaching the exposure control system are dark and offset the tones of the smaller light areas of the subject. As a result, the meter averages these out to what it thinks is a mid tone and over exposes the film so that the dark tones become too light and the light tones are totally over exposed and burned out. A typical example of this would be a single white seagull flying against a background of dark shadowy cliffs. In fact I have just such a sequence on a piece of my own film and all detail in the gull's plumage has been lost because of over-exposure, while the cliffs in the background are a disappointing mid-grey.

At the other extreme, if you are filming a scene with a large area of sky, the meter will be over-influenced by the sky and will close the lens aperture too much resulting in under-exposure of the dark tones. The manual over-ride control enables you to overcome this problem. In the first case, where the meter is tending to over-expose the subject, you will get much better results if you set the over-ride control to give one stop less exposure than the automatic exposure control system recommends. This is usually achieved by moving a small lever to a position marked −1. In the other case, you would move the over-ride control lever to +1 to give one stop more exposure than the automatic system recommends.

Because automatic exposure control systems are designed to average light and dark tones, they produce the best results when your subject is lit from the front or slightly to one side. If the sun is well to one side of the subject, or even directly behind it, the meter in your camera will operate in a similar way to when it sees a predominantly dark subject, because a larger part of the subject will now be in shadow. If this shadowed part of the subject is the most important and you want to see plenty of detail in it, just let the camera's exposure system take care of the situation for you. But if you want to retain the mood of the back-lit subject, throwing the shadowy parts into silhouette, set the manual over-ride to −1 stop again.

Shooting

The first thing you must do when you are ready to start filming is to arrange your subject within the picture format of your film. You do this by looking through the viewfinder. Be sure to place your eye as close as

When you want to retain the mood of a back lit subject, set the manual exposure over-ride to −1 stop

possible to the eyepiece so that you can see the whole picture in the view-finder to avoid having unwanted objects at the edge of the frame. Many cameras are supplied with a rubber eyecup to make this easier and more comfortable.

If your camera is the single lens reflex type, what you see in the view-finder will be exactly what is recorded on the film, but if it is a simpler type of camera, with a separate viewfinder, what you see will be slightly different from what the film sees. For most filming distances, this paral-lax as it is called, will be insignificant, but when you are shooting at dis-tances of five or six feet and closer it can become quite important. You can compensate for parallax, though, by simply moving the camera slightly in the direction of the viewfinder; up if the finder is above the lens or to one side if the finder and the lens are side by side.

Hold it steady

One of the biggest faults in home movies is the jumpy picture, caused by not holding the camera perfectly steady. The instruction manual packed with your camera will give you basic advice on how to hold the camera steady, but here are a few extra tips that you may find useful.

First of all, always hold your movie camera with two hands; it is virtually impossible to keep a camera completely steady if you are only holding it with one. Most movie cameras have some form of pistol grip and I have found the most satisfactory, and certainly the most comfortable, way of holding this type of camera is to hold the pistol grip in my right hand and place my left hand on top of the camera to steady it. Binocular type cameras, such as the Kodak range, are best held . . . just like binoculars! Personally, I find this type of camera less easy to hold perfectly still than the pistol grip type. But no matter what type of grip your camera has, hold the camera firmly against your cheek and tuck your elbows well into your sides to give a solid support. Keep your body steady by spacing your feet slightly apart, making sure that they are on firm ground.

When you press the shutter release to begin filming, do so very gently rather as though you were squeezing the trigger of a rifle. Do not jab at it because this will immediately make the camera jerk and produce a jumpy picture. And if you have been walking up a steep hill or cliff before you shoot your film, give yourself a few minutes let your heartbeat return to normal. I have a film sequence which I shot of the harbour at St Ives in Cornwall from the top of a very long, very steep hill out of the town. When the film is projected the picture jumps very slightly in time with what was a fairly rapid and heavy heart-beat!

An accessory which you will find extremely useful if you get more involved with film making is a good tripod to hold your cine camera perfectly still when you want to take a fairly lengthy sequence from a fixed viewpoint. But buy a good rigid one, preferably with 'U' profile legs rather than telescopic round ones, because the profile type is far less flexible than the tubular type. And choose a tripod with both spike and rubber feet so that you can use it either on smooth floors or on rough ground. You will need to have a pan and tilt head on the tripod for movie work. This is a device which couples the camera to the tripod while still allowing you to turn and tilt the camera both vertically and horizontally, and to do so very smoothly. It also allows you to lock the camera in one direction while still allowing free movement in the other. For example, if you wanted to turn the camera horizontally to pan a

(a) Steady a conventional camera by placing your left hand on top of the camera
(NOTE: My wife, shown here, is left handed!) (b) With binocular type cameras, keep
your elbows well into your side for added stability

A solid tripod with a pan and tilt head is a useful accessory for movie making

wide landscape you could lock the tilt movement. Be careful, though, not to confuse a pan and tilt head with a ball and socket head which is normally used with a still camera. The ball and socket head is quite useless for cine work since it allows the camera to move in all directions and is most difficult to control.

When you are using a cine camera on a tripod with a pan and tilt head, be very careful to set up the tripod so that the camera is perfectly level, otherwise, if you try to pan a shot you will end up with a sloping horizon or tilted buildings.

While a tripod is a useful accessory for general purpose movie work, it becomes absolutely indispensable if you want to shoot close-ups or time-lapse sequences because the slightest movement in shots of this type will completely ruin the whole sequence.

Always use the correct batteries in your camera and keep the contacts on both camera and batteries clean

You are now ready to start shooting some film and in the next chapter I shall explain some of the basic techniques of movie work. But one final point before we move on. Please check that the lens of your movie camera is perfectly clean before you start filming. In fact, carry with you in your camera bag a small, soft camel hair brush with which to dust the lens before you start to film any sequence. If you do this each time the lens should never need any more vigorous cleaning. Dust on the lens will not reduce the sharpness of your pictures very much, but it will reduce the contrast which gives your films sparkle. It is as well, too, to gently brush out the film cartridge compartment of the camera before you load each film. This gets rid of any small particles of film debris.

3 Basic movie technique

How many home movies have you seen where all the family is lined up looking at the camera, standing stock still, just like ordinary holiday snapshot stills? These films ignore the first, the fundamental, and the most important factor about cine photography. When using your cine camera, always remember that it is designed, built, and intended to be used to record movement. Movies should move!

The first thing to remember, then, before you even start to think about the mechanical techniques of zooming, panning, and so on, is to get people who are in your picture to do something. But be sure to make them do it in a natural way – not self-consciously or awkwardly. If the people are children you have no real problem; just get them started on a game of some sort then when they are totally absorbed pick up your movie camera and start shooting. Adults are more difficult; they seem to become self-conscious much more easily than children, but again, if you can get them all interested in something you will solve the biggest part of the problem, especially if they become involved in something which takes all of their attention – surfing, perhaps, or driving a go-kart.

Tell a Story

Your home movies will always be more interesting if, instead of being a disjointed series of shots they can be made to tell a story. If you shoot something that is happening – a motor race, for example – then you will automatically tell a story starting at the beginning with the start of the race, or perhaps preparations before the start, and ending with the winner crossing the line or receiving his prize. Because you film the race as it is happening it will naturally be in the correct sequence. Most short-term happenings you film will tell their own story in this way but when you are dealing with a long-term event, such as a fortnight's holiday, you will have to shoot things as they happen but you may want them in a different sequence when you project the film. This is where editing comes in and I shall be dealing with it at some length later in the book.

Think of your movie camera as a time machine – and that is not as far-fetched as it sounds because a movie camera enables you to control time. For example, it is not very often that you want to film an entire event from start to finish – it would very quickly bore your audience. Instead, you shoot incidents from the event, so when you project the film the event is over in far shorter time than it actually took. In other words, you have, in this case, effectively made time pass more quickly. And if you take a time-lapse sequence of a flower opening you can condense what really takes several hours into a period of a few seconds.

At the other extreme, if your camera has more than one filming speed, enabling you to increase the speed at which the film passes through the camera, you can film sequences in slow motion, thereby effectively stretching time. And the mere fact that you can show a film time after time means that you can, in effect, relive moments that happened months or even years earlier. So you can see that your cine camera really *is* a time machine.

Let us have a look, then, at an example of how your cine camera time machine can tell the story of a whole day out – a visit to the beach, perhaps – in a few minutes' screen time. You would, perhaps, begin your story by showing preparations at home before leaving for the beach. Your wife preparing the food and drinks, packing them into the picnic basket, then with a little help from the children, loading the picnic basket into the boot of the car. When everything is loaded you would shoot a sequence of your wife and children getting into the car, fastening their seat belts and shutting the door. This could then be followed by a shot taken by your wife out of the passenger window of the car showing your house disappearing into the distance as the car pulls away. Next, a few shots taken from the car as you drive along would adequately convey that you were on your journey to your day out by the sea.

When you arrive at the outskirts of the seaside town or village you are visiting, a simple shot of the placename sign followed by a couple of shots as you pass through the village establishes that you have arrived at your destination. The next shot could show your wife and children getting out of the car at the beach car park and, since it is what they usually do, the children running off down the beach to the sea.

The next few sequences in your movie will virtually dictate themselves by the events which happen during that day out by the sea. There

a

(a-d) A typical sequence from a film of a day at the beach. Note the changes of camera angle

b

will be shots such as the children climbing rocks and paddling in the sea,
building sand castles, eating ice creams, and so on. Then there may be a
sequence of your wife relaxing with a book or simply lying in her bikini
sun-bathing, having already done much of the hard work in preparing
the picnic for the day out.

Next comes lunch, with your wife hard at it again cutting bread and
butter, serving salads, cold meat and cheese, pouring coffee from the
flask or boiling water on the portable gas stove. Or maybe that is your
job on a picnic, so get your wife to shoot a short sequence of you boiling
the kettle on the gas stove.

After lunch, when everything has been packed away, and perhaps
loaded back into the car, you may decide to go for a walk along the
beach or on the cliffs, and this may give you the ideal opportunity to
shoot some film of boats in the sea or distant views from the cliff tops.
Perhaps you may also be lucky enough to see some sea birds at close
quarters and shoot some film of them, or if you have a close-up attachment for your movie camera you may be able to get some shots of unusual wild flowers which grow on the cliff tops. At the end of your walk
you may go into a small café or tea shop and a few shots of the family
enjoying buttered scones with jam and cream and a cup of tea will fit in
nicely with the rest of the film.

After that, it is back to the beach again and perhaps a few more shots of

c

d

the children playing in the sea followed, maybe, by a sequence of fishing boats returning and unloading their catch or a cargo of summer visitors who have hoped to catch something.

By now, it is probably getting dusk and it is time to start for home again, but before you do, shoot some film of the family getting back into the car — rather tired by now — and take some final shots of the sunset over the sea to act as a final scene in your movie.

In this way you have probably captured the whole essence of a very enjoyable day by the sea on film using about three cartridges of Super 8 film, making a total screen time of some ten minutes. If you have been careful and selective with the sequences you have filmed, and the length of each shot, you may find that you can join your three cartridges of film together when they come back from processing, into one interesting full-length film. But you are more likely to find that you have made some shots too long and you will need to cut parts from them to make the film more interesting and hold together better. The big problem, then, is to shoot each sequence for just the right length.

Length of Shot

There used to be a general rule of thumb in film making that each different shot should last for about ten seconds. While in some cases this can still apply, it does unfortunately tend to lead to films where one boring ten second sequence is followed by another, and another, and another . . . in fact, ten seconds for most scenes is far too long, the only exceptions being, perhaps, scenes which contain a lot of detail or a lot of action, so that the ten second sequence allows the audience to take in everything that is happening in the picture. If you think about it, ten seconds is quite a long time.

The answer, then, is to match your shot length to the shot itself. In most cases it is sufficient to hold the shot (the term used in cine circles for filming time) for about five to six seconds and only to extend it to say eight or ten seconds when the scene is particularly packed with detail or action. In many cases much shorter shots than five or six seconds will do a particular job more than adequately. This is especially true if you are framing your subject tightly or shooting a close-up. In these cases you may only need to hold the shot for two or three seconds. So, as a general rule, hold long shots for about ten seconds; in exceptional circumstances you may even extend them to twelve or fifteen seconds. Hold medium shots for around six seconds, and close-ups or tightly framed shots for two or three seconds. I shall explain the meanings of long shot, medium shot and close-up shortly.

If you intend to edit your film to its final length by cutting parts from various scenes, as I shall explain in a later chapter, you can add a few seconds on to each sequence that you shoot to allow you to put together the best piece from each sequence for the final film. But be careful not to overdo this; remember that the best editing is always done in the camera, and with film the price it is these days, you can easily find your movie costing you twice as much as it need. Again, a good rule of thumb might be to shoot what will be eventually a six second scene for about eight seconds; this will then leave you thirty-six frames to cut out of that sequence on the editing bench.

But do try to vary the length of your shots; just as the endless sequence of ten second shots that used to form the basic movie can quickly bore your audience, so endless short four or five second shots can quickly make your audience tense and exhausted, while too many long shots of ten to fifteen seconds can actually send them to sleep. However, when you become more experienced in your film making you can actually use these devices to create the mood you want in your audience. For example, using several short tightly framed scenes, one after another to build tension, followed by a single long sequence to allow your audience to relax again.

To begin with, though, try to introduce variety in the length of scene, ideally allowing each scene to remain on the screen just long enough to get its message across to your audience. Remember that each fifty foot cartridge of Super 8 film lasts a total of some four minutes on the screen and if your shot length averages out at eight seconds – that is allowing some short three or four second shots and a few long ten to twelve second ones – you should be able to get around thirty different sequences on each cartridge, and that number of sequences should provide a most interesting four minute movie. However, to begin with you will find it quite difficult to edit your film so precisely in the camera, so be prepared to lose at least a quarter of each cartridge when you edit your film later.

Three Basic Shots

It is very easy when making a movie to forget that, not only can your subject move about, but so can you and your camera. Just as early cine photographers tended to make every sequence last for about ten seconds, they also tended to shoot the whole film with the camera at the same distance from the subject. This again did little to make the film interesting. Fortunately, though, as in most artistic fields, there are a few people who are determined to make their efforts different from everyone else's, and it was so in cine photography; the man who really left his mark in movie making was D.W. Griffith. He realised just how tedious a film can become when it is all shot with the camera at a fixed distance from the subject. So he developed a technique of breaking up an individual sequence into three different types of shot: the long shot, the medium shot, and the close-up. This basic technique of filming has remained unchanged in its concept right up to the present time.

The long shot

The basic idea of the long shot is to locate in general terms where a particular piece of action is taking place and tends, usually, to be rather dull and uninteresting because it is often packed with a lot of small detail and the main subject of the sequence is relegated to a fairly insignificant part of the whole picture. A further problem is that, because the image size on Super 8 film is very small, the mass of detail contained in a long shot tends to become rather fuzzy. For these reasons it is advisable to limit the number of long shots in a Super 8 film to as few as possible. If you do this you have the additional benefit of making long shots more effective when you do use them. If at all possible, try to use your movie camera on a tripod for long shots so that you make the most of every last scrap of sharpness of which your camera's lens is capable.

One particular type of long shot to avoid wherever possible is a long scenic view. While it may look very attractive or even breathtaking while you are standing looking at it, when it appears on the screen it can be quite boring for the audience, because it will generally be packed with fine detail but have very little action or possibly none at all. So to the audience it will appear just like a ten second shot of a picture postcard. If you want to include a scene of this type in your movie, shoot for

Long shot

Medium shot

two or three seconds and then arrange for someone to walk into the scene to add a little movement and interest. But have the person look at the scene rather than at the camera or your scenic view will suddenly become a picture of a person with a pretty background. Another useful trick for this type of shot is to shoot it through a foreground of moving leaves or long grasses; this is usually sufficient to relieve the inherent stillness of a long shot.

Medium shot

When talking about Super 8 movie films, the medium shot is that which you take at a distance of around ten feet from your subject. This is sufficient to ensure that the subject is sharp and that all detail is clearly visible.

While the long shot has established the general location of any action that is taking place, the medium shot should move in on the main subject of the action so that the audience is left in no doubt as to what is the main subject of the sequence. Try to make the medium shot follow the long shot as smoothly as possible. You will, of course, have to move in closer to your subject for the medium shot and at this stage it is better to do so physically rather than by zooming in using your zoom lens. The reason for this is that by physically moving closer to your subject you can also change the angle from which you shoot to give added interest to the film.

If you think about it, taking a long shot from one position then simply walking a few feet forward to take the medium shot is going to produce the effect of a jump on the screen when the film is projected. It is much better to move to one side or the other slightly as you move forward so that the action takes place in a slightly different direction in the medium shot than it did in the long shot. By doing this, the whole sequence can be made to flow smoothly together rather than appear as a series of jerky snapshots.

If your movie camera is fitted with a zoom lens, I have found it better to use the lens towards its telephoto end for the medium shot because the depth of field is shallower at a long focal length than it is at a short one, and this has the very useful effect of throwing the background out of focus and allowing the audience to concentrate on the main subject of

the shot. But this obviously only applies if the lens on your movie camera
is of variable focus. Another advantage that using the zoom lens towards
the telephoto end of its travel gives is that it enables you to frame your
picture more tightly to concentrate the attention of the audience on what
you are filming.

The close-up shot

Close-up shots are the ones that really make a film. They take your audience right into the heart of the action with all superfluous detail removed
from the shot. Generally speaking, the greater the number of close-ups
you can get into your movie, the more interesting and effective that
movie will be. And do not forget that the close-up need only be held for
a second or two, yet during that very short time it can make more impact
than a five or six second medium shot. For example, if you are filming
someone playing golf, a close-up shot of the club actually hitting the
ball, and lasting perhaps only one second, can have far more excitement
than a shot of the entire swing lasting several seconds.

Shots like this can often be dropped into a sequence and really build up
the excitement of the whole movie. But while close-up shots can be truly
effective in a movie, they must be shot with impeccable technique or
they can do just the opposite and ruin the film. To begin with, you must
hold the camera absolutely still. In fact it is a very good idea to have the
camera mounted firmly on a tripod for all close-up shots wherever possible, because nothing looks worse on the screen than a close-up shot
which is jumping about all over the place. A close-up shot must also be
critically sharp, which means that you must take your time over focusing
accurately if your camera has a variable focus lens. However, it is possible to shoot close-ups while hand-holding the camera, it just takes a
little more practice and patience. Again, as with the medium shot, when
you move in close to your subject, to make a close-up shot, change the
camera angle slightly to add even more interest to the film.

These three basic shots – the long shot, the medium shot, and the close-
up – are the bones on which to build any movie film. The way you use
them is entirely up to you. The usual sequence is to start with a long shot,
move in to a medium shot, and finish on a close-up. But simply because
this is what is usually done, it can often pay dividends to change the

Close up

sequence. For example, there is no reason at all why you should not start with a close-up shot, move back to a long shot, and finish the sequence by moving back to a medium shot or even another close-up shot. The only way that you can learn to string your three basic shots together in the most effective way is by looking at as many professional films as you can – television is a very good source, of course – and by shooting as much film yourself as you can.

Direction of Movement

When you are shooting a film sequence using the three basic shots, one thing that is vitally important is to maintain the direction of movement on the screen. For instance, if the first shot in your sequence – maybe the long shot – shows the action starting in the right hand side of the picture frame, and moving left, make sure that the next shot also has the action moving from right to left. Continue to maintain this direction of movement for the whole sequence unless you allow the direction of movement to change during one of the shots that you film. If you do so, then make sure that the next shot shows the action moving in the new direction on the screen.

This maintaining of screen direction is one of the traps that it is all too easy to fall into when making your early films. But it is one which can be easily avoided if you think about what you are going to shoot before you actually press the shutter release. A film sequence which starts with the action moving from right to left followed by a new shot where the action moves from left to right and finishing with a third sequence with the action going from right to left again can at best be confusing. At worst it can reduce what would have been an entertaining film into an object of ridicule.

Changing direction

It is very simple to establish a change of direction on the screen. If, for instance, you are filming a car travelling along a street and you want to indicate that it turns to the right or the left, into another street, it is quite sufficient to show the beginning of the change of direction. There is no need to show the entire operation, because that would use up far too much film. So the next shot can show the car travelling in a new direction, as long as it is the direction established by the change in the previous shot. For example, if the car is travelling directly towards you and turns off to your right, it will leave the frame on the right hand side. For the second shot, therefore, you must cross over the road and pick up the car again as it enters the top of the frame and starts to come towards you again. When this sequence is shown on the screen it looks quite normal to the audience because they have seen the car turn to the right as it approached the camera and they are therefore prepared when in the second shot it appears at the top of the frame turning towards the camera and then heading straight for the camera once again. The idea of crossing over the road is to enable you to change the camera angle as well as the direction in which the car is moving to give added interest to the sequence. You can of course shoot the sequence without crossing to the other side of the road.

One fairly common change of direction which needs to be established is when someone moves from one side of a door to the other. You may, for instance, be shooting a film of some children at play which starts when a neighbour's child comes to call for your little boy or girl. You could start the film with a shot of the neighbour's child knocking your front door, holding the shot until the front door just begins to open. This is then followed by a shot taken from the other side of the door, inside your house, of your wife opening the door to see the neighbour's child standing there. Your wife would then invite the child in and by this simple sequence you have changed the action from an outside shot to an inside one.

Cutaways

There is one other basic technique which comes into changing direction and which you can use to great effect in your movies: the cutaway. What this means is simply that when you are filming an event you leave the main action of the event very briefly to show some other aspect that is linked to the main action but is quite different. A typical example might be when you are filming a motor race. To relieve what can become a tedious sequence of one car following another speeding round the track, you can periodically cut away to the reaction of the spectators. In this way you can prevent your audience becoming bored and add interest and a little variety to the main story.

4 The camera in action

In the last chapter I dealt with the three basic types of shot and how to link them together to form an interesting film. Now I shall move on a little further to talk about moving the camera itself during filming. In technical terms, the four basic ways in which you can do this are panning, tilting, zooming, and tracking. All four are much easier to carry out if you have the camera firmly mounted on a tripod. But with a little practice you can achieve fairly good results with the camera hand-held. The only problem will be that you are unlikely to get such a smooth result.

The biggest danger when using any of the four moving camera techniques is to carry out the action too quickly. Done properly, any or all of these moving camera techniques can lift an ordinary movie into something fairly spectacular.

Panning

The main purpose of panning in movie making is to keep a moving object centred in the frame. A typical example is a racing car moving past you at fairly high speed. The idea is to pick up the car when it is some considerable distance from you and to move the camera, keeping the car centred in the viewfinder, as it passes you. If you are using your camera on a tripod, you simply level the camera, lock the tilt movement of the pan and tilt head, and follow the action of the car by swinging the pan arm. But if you are using the camera hand held, you will need to take a little more trouble over the shot. Hold the camera in a comfortable position with your arms well into your sides, as I explained in chapter 2, and plant your feet firmly on the ground, slightly apart. Swing your body from the waist, moving only fast enough to keep the moving car centred in the viewfinder. Concentrate on swinging in a smooth continuous arc, otherwise when the film is projected the subject will appear to jump about all over the screen. If your panning has been carried out successfully, the result on the screen will be a fast moving, perfectly sharp car

You will need to develop smooth panning for filming fast action sports

against a blurred background which enhances the feeling of speed in the shot.

The length of a panning sequence will obviously depend on the time it takes for the event to happen. For example, take the racing car; if it takes five seconds for the racing car to complete its journey past you, then the length of the pan shot to film that racing car must be five seconds. But where you have a choice, it is better to keep a pan sequence of moving action fairly short, if only to reduce the risk of camera shake.

Similarly, the effective focal length of the lens you use – that is the position in which you set your zoom lens – will depend to some extent on how far away the action is happening. If you are having to use the lens very near to its maximum telephoto position, a tripod becomes, in my opinion, virtually indispensable, if you are to achieve a smooth pan: it is very difficult to produce a smooth pan hand-held with anything over a very mild telephoto length – say about 15mm focal length.

Panoramic views

Without doubt, one of the most boring of sequences in many home movies is a scenic pan. Yet it is easy to see why so many of these shots are taken; when you come across a scene of great beauty the temptation is to try to include as much of that scene in your movie as possible. Obviously you cannot get it all into a single shot, so you start to pan from one side, moving the camera round to include the whole of the panoramic view. And when it is projected on to the screen the view seems to have lost all the magic it had when you shot the film.

When you come across a situation like this, look carefully at the view before you start to shoot and ask yourself whether the *whole* view is necessary to convey the feeling of natural beauty. In most cases the answer will be no. Instead you will be able to isolate two or three particular areas which will get across the feeling that you have for the view far more effectively than panning around the whole lot. However, if you feel that you really must use a pan shot, this is the way to do it.

Start by shooting the extreme left hand side of the scene, holding the camera still for about two seconds, then pan *very very slowly* and *very very smoothly* across the rest of the view. When you reach the right hand extreme of the view, hold the shot for about two or three seconds. And do not commit the cardinal sin of panning quickly backwards and forwards across the scene, looking at different parts as they take your eye. The result of this on the screen can only be described as disastrous.

One way in which you can make a panoramic view more interesting is by combining a panning action and a zooming action. Before you start to shoot the sequence pick out an interesting object in the view – a waterfall, maybe – pan round to this from your chosen starting point then hold the shot for a couple of seconds before zooming very slowly into the waterfall to finish with a close-up which you then hold for two or three seconds again. At this point you can, if you like, stop shooting, go back to your long shot, pan round a little further until you come to another interesting object, then zoom in on that in the same way.

One thing to bear in mind about panning, whether it be for action shots or for panoramic views, is not to use the technique too much. You have probably seen home movies which consist of one pan shot followed by another – usually at too great a speed – and you all know what the result is on the screen. So before you begin to film a pan shot, ask yourself whether the scene could not be better filmed in another way. By shooting a series of straight shots, for example.

There is one instance where you can break the basic rule of panning (doing it slowly) and that is when you want to move rapidly from one location to another. The way this is usually done in professional films is by dissolving one scene into the other so that they merge into one another. But while a few of the more expensive amateur cine cameras have the facility to make dissolve shots a great many more do not, so an alternative way of moving from one location to another is by using what is called a zip pan or blur pan. The idea is to pan very quickly so that the subject becomes completely blurred, then you stop shooting, change to the new scene, and when you begin shooting again you start by panning very quickly, slowing down until the camera comes to rest on the new scene. The result on the screen is that one location starts to pan slowly, then becomes a blur, slowing down again and finally stopping at the new location, providing a very unusual transition from one scene to another. But be warned: only use it once in any film. Like any other novel device, overuse lessens its impact.

When you are shooting this kind of zip pan it is as well to make the blurred section fairly long so that you can cut it to the most effective length later when you come to edit your film.

Tilting

The only difference between panning and tilting is that while panning takes place horizontally, tilting takes place vertically. It can be quite useful when you are shooting film of a fairly tall building; you can start at the bottom of the building and move slowly up until you reach the top. But again, like panning, you must carry out this operation very slowly. And, of course, it sometimes makes an interesting change if you start at the top of the building and pan down it.

As with panning shots, begin the sequence by holding the shot still for two or three seconds before beginning the tilt and finish with a two or three second hold again with the camera still.

A variation of the tilt movement is known in professional circles as craning. This simply means that the camera moves up or down vertically but without actually tilting. Professional studios use a special camera stand which moves the camera smoothly under power, but it is possible to simulate this with a hand held camera. You begin by crouching in a knees bend position, holding the camera perfectly level, then slowly straighten your legs while shooting the film. This will give you a craning action of about five feet, depending, of course, on your height. It is necessary to practice this action a great deal before using it to shoot film, because it is not at all easy to raise the camera in this way perfectly smoothly, and if you cannot do it smoothly it is better not to attempt it at all. An alternative way of craning is easier to achieve if you have a tripod with a geared centre column. You simply start with the column at the bottom of its travel and slowly wind it up. But be sure that your tripod really is steady and that the column does not tend to twist as it rises or the effect on the screen will not be at all what you intended.

Zooming

Without doubt, the development of the zoom lens for amateur cine cameras has been one of the greatest steps forward in recent years. Unfortunately, it has also been responsible to some extent for a deterioration in the quality of home movies. A great many amateurs, when they start to use their cine camera with a zoom lens seem to think that every sequence they shoot must make use of the zoom facility. So every cartridge of film contains at least half a dozen sequences zooming in on a subject or zooming out from one. Yet used properly, the zoom lens brings advanced movie making techniques within easy grasp of the beginner.

The zoom lens is, in effect, a lens of infinitely variable focal length between two fixed extremes. Medium priced cine cameras usually have a zoom range of about 3:1. In other words, if the minimum focal length is 9mm, the longest would be 27mm. But many others are available with zoom ratios of 4:1, 5:1, even as high as 10:1. The biggest advantage of a zoom lens is not the fact that it enables you to change the size of the subject within your picture while you are filming, but that it enables you to make the subject exactly the size you want within the frame before you start filming. It enables you to fill the frame with your subject. The fact that you can change the image size during filming should be regarded as a bonus rather than as a fundamental necessity of using a zoom lens.

Before I deal with actually zooming the lens during filming, I am going to say a little about using it in its telephoto and wide angle positions.

Telephoto

When your zoom lens is set at its maximum telephoto position, it enables you to take close-up views of objects at a considerable distance, and this makes it ideal for subjects such as wild birds or animals and sports where you are necessarily at some distance from the action – a typical example is motor racing. The big thing to remember when you are using your cine camera in its telephoto mode is to keep it absolutely still. Because you are in effect magnifying the size of the subject within the frame, you are also magnifying by the same amount any movement of the camera. So for extreme telephoto shots always try to use the camera fixed firmly to a tripod.

Another characteristic of the telephoto lens, or the zoom lens in its telephoto position, is that depth of field is reduced considerably. This means that if your lens is of a variable focus type, you must be particularly careful to focus accurately on your subject.

The telephoto lens gives an apparent distortion of perspective – the relationship of the size of objects at different distances from the camera one to another – by making these objects appear much closer together than they really are. This can create quite spectacular effects in some circumstances; for instance, taking a piece of film of a cricket match from directly behind the batsman. When the bowler makes his run to deliver the ball the fact that the effective distance between the bowler and the batsman has been reduced by the telephoto lens can produce a quite terrifying result!

Wide angle

The basic use of the zoom lens at its wide angle setting is to enable you to fit more into the picture area than you would normally be able to do. This is particularly useful when you are filming in rather cramped situations where you cannot move any further back from your subject. But like the telephoto, the wide angle lens also introduces distortion into the picture, although in this case it appears to increase the distance between different objects in the picture simply because to make an object sufficiently large in the viewfinder you need to move closer to it and this increases the perspective to make more distant objects appear comparatively smaller.

While the telephoto lens is ideal for taking close-up pictures of people, the wide angle lens comes into its own for taking full length shots. In fact, if you try to use it for close-up pictures of faces you will find that the face tends to become distorted due to the close distance at which you have to work from your subject in order to fill the frame.

If you use your zoom lens to give you just telephoto, just wide angle, and just normal shots instead of zooming in and out on your subjects at every opportunity, you will find that you can introduce a very pleasing variety of shots into your film and make the whole movie far more interesting.

Active zooming

There is no doubt at all that a zoom shot – from wide angle to telephoto in one long sequence – can produce really spectacular results – if you use it sparingly. Unfortunately, far too many amateur film makers tend to use the zoom technique for practically every shot they make, and this can produce dull repetitive filming and, incidentally, waste an awful lot of expensive film. I would suggest, in fact, that if you have two action zoom shots on a single fifty foot cartridge of film you have enough, and in many cases, more than enough. Used sparingly the zoom shot can really concentrate the attention of your audience on to your subject, but use it too much and it loses its effect.

Of course, you can always use the zoom sequence the other way round, starting with a tight close-up shot and opening out into a wide angle long shot to put the main subject into its proper location. The zoom shot really is one occasion when the tripod becomes almost indispensable because instead of being able to hold your camera firmly with both hands, you have to use one of your hands to operate the zoom control. This inevitably means that you cannot hold the camera quite as still. However, if you do not have a tripod you can always improvise by resting the camera on the top of a wall or a gate, or even pressing it up against the side of a tree. But whatever you do, make sure that you hold the camera as steady as you possibly can.

Unfortunately, an increasing number of movie cameras these days have a power zoom. Now you may think that this is a very good idea, and so it is in some instances. But it has one big disadvantage; it means that the speed at which you zoom is controlled by the camera mechanism rather than by yourself. In most cases you want to zoom fairly slowly to

a

b

(a-h) A typical zoom sequence using a 4:1 zoom range (equivalent to about 7mm – 28mm)

Note: This series of pictures was taken with a 35mm Praktica SLR camera fitted with a Sigma 39–80mm zoom lens and, for some of the shots, a 2x converter. The reason for this is that it is not possible to reproduce sufficiently high quality in print from Super 8 shots

c

d

e

f

g

h

allow your audience time to take in what is happening, but there are times when, for dramatic effect, you may want to zoom extremely rapidly from a wide angle shot to an extreme telephoto. Unless your power zoom camera has a manual over-ride, you cannot do this.

Generally speaking, the best way to shoot a zoom sequence is to start with one or two seconds with the lens in its wide angle position (or telephoto if you are doing a reverse zoom) and then start to zoom very slowly and at the end leave the close-up (or long shot) on the screen for two or three seconds. This method of working enables your audience to become aware of the initial location of the shot and leaves them with a lasting impression of the close-up at the end of the sequence.

Another fault which many amateur cine photographers seem to have is to think that they have to use the full extent of the zoom range for every zoom shot they take. Again, in many cases, using the zoom over its full range can be most effective, but in other cases you may need only to work over a very limited range – perhaps a ratio of 2:1 instead of the 5:1 or more of which the total zoom range is capable. The reason for this limited zoom is quite simple; in some cases, if you start at the full wide angle of which the zoom is capable, you may find that your subject is so small as to virtually disappear in the surrounding location, and when you show the film on the screen you may find that you have wasted half the footage because you could have started the zoom at less of a wide angle and saved yourself a considerable amount of film. So the best thing to do is to try out the zoom you intend to make without running the camera so that you can see exactly how the sequence will appear on the screen. Then, if you are satisfied with it, repeat the zoom with the camera running.

I have already mentioned the speed of zooming and here again there can be no hard and fast rules – the speed of zoom depends entirely on the effect you are trying to achieve. However, in most cases a fairly slow change from wide angle to telephoto or telephoto to wide angle will give you the best results. But if you are zooming in from a wide angle shot of a landscape to a single feature of that landscape, please make sure that the view itself is interesting enough to hold the attention of the audience over the entire sequence of the zoom.

One way you can create tremendous impact with a zoom lens is by zooming from wide angle to telephoto very quickly while filming a moving object such as a car which is travelling directly towards you. The effect of such a sequence on the screen can be quite rivetting.

You can often make a zoom sequence more interesting and effective if you include some static object towards the edge of the picture when you are at the wide angle end of the zoom lens travel. Then when you begin to zoom in towards your subject you will create the impression of the camera itself moving rather than just pulling a distant view closer to you. Remember that a zoom lens used intelligently can be one of the most valuable features of your cine camera. But try to use it imaginatively rather than simply zooming in and out on every shot you take. Invest a few cartridges of film in experimenting with your zoom lens. It will cost you a few pounds, but it will be money well spent because it will enable you to save film in future filming, rather than wasting it.

Tracking

One of the big problems with zoom lenses is that they tend to make you lazy. You can effectively move in on a subject by simply turning the zoom control on your camera without having to move at all. Because of this, the tracked shot has virtually disappeared from the amateur film maker's repertoire. Which is a pity, because the tracked shot offers features which zooming simply cannot achieve.

The difference between a tracked shot and a zoom shot is that while you move in effectively on your subject with a zoom lens, but without actually changing position, in a tracked shot you physically move towards the subject. The difference on the screen is subtle but significant. When you track in on your subject, the subject becomes larger in the viewfinder and the background becomes relatively smaller, as the result of the gradual change in perspective caused by moving closer to the subject. In a zoom shot, however, the actual perspective does not change because you remain at a fixed distance from your subject, and all that happens in fact is that the subject becomes larger on the screen while foreground and background objects remain in the same proportion one to the other. The tracked shot becomes very effective when you are looking at a subject and you want to get closer to it just as you would if you were looking at it with your eyes rather than with a movie camera.

In other words, if you are looking at an object on the ground and you would normally bend down to get a better view of it, by tracking the camera down towards the object you can reproduce this effect on the screen much more effectively than by zooming on to it. It should be carried out fairly slowly so that it appears to the audience when shown on the screen as a natural movement.

Tracked shots can also be effectively used if you are moving forward, such as along a street or through a gate into a field on a nature walk perhaps. In this case the effect is of looking at the scene through the eyes of a character in your movie. One big advantage of the tracked shot over the zoom is that it tends not to become tedious quite so quickly. But it takes quite a lot of practice to get a tracked shot really smooth if you are walking with the camera while filming, because you tend to get a certain amount of sway as you walk. In some cases this does not matter too much if you intend the shot to appear as through the eyes of a character in the movie, but again, as with zoom shots, practise with a few lengths of odd film to find out how to handle the technique most effectively.

5 Getting more ambitious

Modern Super 8 movie cameras are far more versatile than were amateur cine cameras of a few years ago, and the introduction of high speed movie films has made them even more so. All this means that you can now do far more with your movie camera than you would have been able to do ten years ago. One of the ways in which this increased versatility has been most obvious is in filming indoors.

With the combination of wide aperture lenses on modern cine cameras and using a high speed film such as Ektachrome 160 Type A, you will often find that you can film indoors without the need to use special lighting, and this, in most cases, is all to the good because filming in normal domestic lighting conditions means that you retain the character of the situation. The lighting you see on the screen is the same as the lighting in the room when it is in normal use.

The only problem is that because your eyes adjust themselves automatically to varying brightnesses of light, the difference between the brightness of a dining table, for example, lit directly from above and a cupboard a few feet away from the table and which is in shadow, may in fact be quite considerable. While your eye does not notice this too much because of its ability to compensate for different brightnesses, the effect will show up on film. The automatic exposure system of your camera will probably set the exposure midway between the brightly lit table and the shadowy cupboard and the result may well be burned-out highlights around the table and blocked-up shadows at the cupboard. The best way to overcome this is to frame your picture more tightly so that you do not have these extremes of light and dark in the shot at the same time.

However, if you must have both bright highlights and deep shadows in the same shot you will have to decide which are the more important and use the manual exposure over-ride lever on the camera to compensate. If you decide that the highlights are more important you will need to set the over-ride control to $-\frac{1}{2}$ or -1, while if the shadows are more important you must set it at $+\frac{1}{2}$ or $+1$.

Using Supplementary Lighting

If you want to make a lot of movies indoors you will probably buy some form of photographic lighting system to enable you to increase the level of illumination in the room and to balance the brightness ratio between the highlights and shadows so that the film can cope with them. But look carefully before you buy your lighting system; there are a great many on the market which are designed to fix on to the camera rather like a flash-gun fits on to a still camera. Now this is all very well in that it provides you with a fairly compact single unit which both lights the subject and films it, but from an aesthetic point of view, mounting the lighting unit on the camera itself is the worst possible thing you can do. In the first place it tends to over-illuminate objects in the foreground and under il-luminate those at the back. And if you are filming people you tend to produce results with flat, pasty white faces which have no shape to them because there is no modelling caused by the soft shadows cast by the cheekbones. Finally, because the lamps get very hot you will quickly find that both yourself and the people you are filming become rather fed up with the whole thing. All this seems to indicate that movie lights are not really very much use at all, but if supplementary lighting is used properly it can provide very satisfactory results.

The first way to start producing good results from supplementary lighting is to get the lights away from the camera. A good starting point is to place the lights to one side of the camera and somewhat above it so that they shine down and slightly from one side on to the subject. And if you use a lamp with a large reflector, the lighting produced will be soft and will not cast harsh shadows. Of course, by removing the light from the camera you will be able to move about much more freely around your subject to produce different camera angles.

Many people advise using more than one light source to ensure that no part of the subject is in deep shadow and to make sure that there is sufficient light for successful filming. I am afraid I disagree; I am strictly a one light source man and if there are any shadows to be lightened I prefer to use large sheets of white card or polystyrene as reflectors to push some light back into the shadows. My reason for this is very simple: if you use more than one light source you are in constant danger

Paterson lighting units for filming indoors

of producing multiple shadows on your subject, one from each light source. By using reflectors, however, you can never put enough light into the subject from the reflectors to overcome the brightness of the main light and so cause crossed shadows. If you watch some of the very early Hollywood movies which are sometimes shown on television these days, you will see exactly what I mean; there are some sequences, allegedly shot outdoors, where there must be at least three suns in the sky! As for the other reason for using more than one light – to produce sufficient light to enable successful filming to take place – modern cine camera design and the advent of faster films has largely counteracted this.

If you have a large area to light, the best way of doing it is by bouncing the light from your one lamp from the ceiling. To do this you simply point the light source at the ceiling instead of at the subject and the whole of the ceiling becomes one large diffuse light source. The advantage of doing this is that the light spreads over a much larger area and produces very few shadows, and those shadows are soft enough not to cause problems of contrast on the film. Incidentally, one thing you must remember to do when filming indoors with artificial light is to remove the built-in filter from behind the lens by operating the filter lever on your camera. If you intend to shoot sequences near a window where you have both daylight and artificial light from inside the room, use Ektachrome 160 Type G film to avoid colour casts in your finished movie.

To go back for a moment to what I said at the beginning of this short section, I feel that, if at all possible, it is much better to shoot your films indoors using the normal existing lighting within the room where you film. In this way the resulting movie will always look more natural and retain more character than one which has obviously been lit artificially.

Shooting Close-ups

In this context, what I mean by close-ups is not a close shot as I described in chapter 3, but an extreme close-up of, perhaps, the inside of a flower, a small piece of machinery such as a watch, an insect, or any other similar very small object. Having defined the close-up, I must now say, right at the start, that unless you have a movie camera with a reflex view-finder system and variable focus lens, you will find it extremely difficult to shoot this type of close-up. Not impossible, but difficult.

Without reflex viewfinding, the lens of your cine camera and the viewfinder see slightly different views of the subject, as I explained earlier in the book, and when you are filming at extremely close distances this parallax becomes very significant indeed. But even if you do own a simple movie camera without variable focus and without reflex viewfinding, you can still shoot close-up film even though it becomes a little more difficult. You can solve the focusing problem by using supplementary close-up lenses which enable you to get much closer to your subject and still keep the subject sharply in focus. These close-up lenses come in various powers identified by a dioptre number. If you buy one each of +1, +2, and +3 dioptre, you will find that they enable you to shoot subjects down to a distance of about thirteen inches. And if your camera has a zoom lens you can increase the apparent size of the objects still further by setting the zoom lens to its maximum telephoto position. A table of close-up distances and the areas covered by the various zoom lens settings is included in the appendices at the end of this book.

The problem of parallax is a little more difficult to overcome, but not much. All you need is a piece of stiff card or thin plywood for each of the close-up lenses you buy. Cut the card to exactly the length of the subject distance given in the close-up tables I have just mentioned and make the width of the card the same as the area width which you can also get from the table. Now draw a line down the centre of the length of the card and you have a simple but effective device which will enable you to set up your camera at exactly the right distance and with the subject in exactly the right position for filming.

Even if your cine camera is fitted with a focusing lens you will probably still need to use supplementary lenses with it to enable you to get close enough to your subject; but used in conjunction with the focusing system and the telephoto setting of your zoom lens, you will find that you can produce quite large images in the viewfinder.

One of the biggest problems in shooting close-ups is that the depth of field, or zone of sharpness, becomes very shallow at close distances, so if your camera has a focusing movement on the lens you must be sure that the subject is very accurately focused, and if it is a fixed focus lens you must measure the distance very carefully using a tape measure or the close-up device I have just described. And because depth of field is also

Small pieces of machinery such as a watch make fascinating close ups in cine

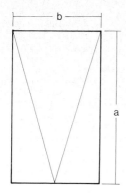

A simple board with dimension 'a' equal to the focusing distance and 'b' equal to the width of subject at that distance. Place the camera lens (with close-up lens fitted) at the point of the 'V'

shallow with wide lens apertures, and therefore when the lighting is fairly dull, you should aim to have a fairly bright light source illuminating your subject so that the automatic exposure system of the camera sets the lens at a reasonably small aperture for maximum depth of field. So it is best to limit your close-up filming outdoors to days when there is plenty of bright sunlight falling on your subject and use white card reflectors to throw a little more light into the shadow areas.

Indoors the problem is a little more difficult, because to get sufficient light on to the subject means that you have to use fairly bright light sources quite close to the subject and this in turn means that there is a danger of the subject becoming overheated. The best compromise is to use a directional light source, such as a reading lamp, in conjunction with a high speed movie film. Again you can use white card reflectors to increase the amount of light on the subject or use small handbag mirrors which provide a more directional supplementary light.

If your movie camera has a cable release socket you will find it a great advantage for close-up work because it enables you to start and stop the camera without actually touching the camera. And when you are working at such close distances from your subject even the very slight movement that can be caused by pressing the shutter release will record quite markedly on the film and this, of course, will show as a jerk on the screen when you project the film.

If you are shooting close-ups of flowers outside, the wind can provide quite a problem, since even the lightest breeze can cause a relatively large movement of the flower within the film frame. If your movie camera has two or three filming speeds you can minimise this problem by filming at a slightly higher speed – say 24 or even 32 fps – instead of the normal 18 fps. This has the effect, when you show the film, of slowing down any movement caused by the breeze to the point where it is not so distracting for the audience. But if your camera has just the one speed you can minimise the effects of the breeze by pegging a piece of clear acetate in a semicircle around the sides and back of the subject to act as a wind-break; it will, of course, have no effect on the lighting of your subject and since it is transparent it should be quite invisible in the finished shot.

Titling

Nothing adds a touch of professionalism to a home movie more easily than an attractive title at the beginning and end of your film. The easy way out is to buy ready-made titles which are available at many photographic shops in standard forms like 'Our Holiday', 'Christmas Party', and so on. But these ready-made titles are rarely produced very imaginatively and it is much better – and much more satisfying – to produce your own. And it is not very difficult, especially if you have a close-up lens attachment for your movie camera.

The two main titles that you need to make for a movie are a phrase to sum up the movie which can act as the main title, and a simple statement to finish the film off – 'The End'. Some advanced amateurs produce other titles which say that the film has been produced and directed by Bill Bloggs, but I must confess that I find this sort of thing rather pretentious.

By far the biggest danger when making a title for the film is to try to include too many words; after all, why try to tell the whole story in the title when you have the movie itself to do that for you?

Let us take a specific example. Assume, for instance, that you have made a movie of your 1976 holiday in Wales. Instead of simply calling it 'Our Holiday, 1976', which, let us face it, is not going to instil a great deal of enthusiasm in any audience, why not call it 'A Summer in Wales', or 'The Land of Song', or even 'Welcome to Wales'. In all of these titles you are saying rather more than that the film is a record of

A simple titling set-up. A close-up lens would need to be fitted to the cine camera

your holiday; you are immediately telling your audience where that holiday took place.

If the holiday film tends to cover one particular aspect – perhaps country crafts or the weaving of Welsh tweed – you could edit the film to produce a more interesting movie dealing with just that aspect and disregard the fact that it was filmed on holiday altogether. In this case the title for the film might be 'Country Crafts of Wales'.

In some cases you can find your titles ready-made in the form of road signs or perhaps the cover of a book. To go back to the original Welsh example again; I have spent several holidays in Wales and on the route that I generally take from my home in the Midlands, at the point where I enter Wales there is a road sign which says 'Welcome to Wales' in both English and Welsh. I have photographed this particular road sign and it now forms the title for one of my movies. You can make similar titles from other signs; for example, if you are making a movie about a nature trail you will often find the start of the trail signposted and this will form a ready-made title for the movie.

Another fairly simple and straightforward method of making a title for a holiday film is to print the title in the sand on the beach and film that. This not only tells the audience that the film is about a holiday, but that it is about a seaside holiday. Incidentally, you can finish a seaside movie quite effectively by writing the words 'The End' in the sand on the beach and then waiting until the tide starts to come in and shoot the title as the sea begins to wash the lettering away. This can form quite an attractive end to a holiday movie.

But however you make your title, the length of the shot is quite important. It is one of the few occasions when you should not be in too much of a hurry to finish the sequence. In fact, a good general rule is to allow twice as long as it takes you to read the title.

If you are going to make your titles right from scratch, one interesting and attractive way of doing so is to use plastic letters which are sold for the purpose by many photographic dealers. You can lay them out on a sheet of black, white or coloured paper and film them with the camera attached to a tripod or copying stand above the title. To make it more interesting you can set out these plastic letters on a map of the area where your holiday took place: you will need a map or piece of paper about 13

Use ready-made titles where suitable

× 18 inches if you are filming at a distance of about three feet. Obviously, with close-up lenses which enable you to shoot closer than this the size of the paper or map can be reduced and if you have a zoom lens on your camera you can adjust the final framing by adjusting the effective focal length.

Special movie titlers are available, but it is quite easy to make one for yourself from a flat piece of wood which acts as a camera platform with a second piece of wood to act as a title board fixed horizontally to it. Make the platform about six inches wide and slightly longer than the camera to subject distance necessary to shoot the title: you can find out what this distance is from the close-up tables in the appendices at the back of this book.

As an example, if you are using a +2 dioptre close-up lens on a camera with a 13mm fixed focus lens the distance between the camera and the title board must be $17\frac{1}{2}$ inches, so you would make the camera platform somewhat longer than this to enable you to fix the camera and the title board to the platform.

Make the title board about 10 × 8 inches to give you plenty of room to attach the background and lettering. You may have to build up the part of the camera platform where the camera is attached so that the height of the lens above the platform is the same as the centre of the title board. When you mark out the position of the title on the board make sure that the centre of the title is directly opposite the centre of the camera lens – assuming, of course, that you do not want an intentionally off-centre title. And unless you have a reflex type of movie camera do not rely on the optical viewfinder of the camera for centering the title.

As far as backgrounds are concerned, you can use any plain colour of card or you can use a colour print from one of your still photographs. An alternative possibility is to make the background from a sheet of stiff matt acetate or tracing paper and to project a suitable scene from one of your movies on to this sheet from behind, with the lettering attached to the front of the sheet. This way you can make a title with a moving background which can look very professional indeed when shown on the screen.

One very easy way of making your own titles is to use instant lettering such as Letraset. You can apply this direct to a piece of plain coloured card or, if you want to superimpose the title over a still photograph or a back-projected piece of film as I have just described, you can assemble the lettering on a sheet of clear acetate which you then suspend in front of the chosen background.

Personally, I believe that a simple straightforward typeface is the best for making movie titles, but for the odd occasion when you want something really different you can choose a more unusual typeface. Or you can even make your letters out of natural objects such as small pebbles, sea shells, or small flower heads. If your camera has the facility for making single frame exposures you can make your title spell itself out on the screen. What you do is place the first letter in position and shoot two or three frames, then place the second letter in position and shoot another two or three frames, place the third letter in position, and so on until the

Sunsets make a spectacular finishing shot for a holiday film and are easy to shoot

full title is spelled out. But this is not something to do on every film otherwise it quickly becomes tedious.

Sunsets

One of the most attractive ways of finishing a movie, especially one which has dealt with a holiday, is with a sequence of a sunset which can provide a spectacular climax to the film. Many amateur cine photographers seem to be apprehensive about trying to film a sunset, yet in fact nothing could be simpler. With the automatic exposure control fitted to most cameras these days all you do is simply point the camera at the sunset and press the button; as long as the sun is fairly low down towards the horizon the automatic exposure given will be just about right. And in any case, it is not all that critical.

One word of advice, though, is to have some sort of recognisable object, such as a boat or a group of people, in the immediate foreground to add depth to the sunset scene. Because the camera sets the exposure on the much brighter sunset itself, these objects or people will become silhouettes. And if you really want to add impact set your zoom lens to its maximum telephoto position so that the disc of the sun becomes really large in the picture area.

Playing About with Time

I said earlier that you can regard your cine camera as a time machine and I now want to explain briefly how you can do this. I have mentioned the relatively simple techniques of filming scenes in slow motion or at increased speed. By merely selecting a faster filming, speed sequences can be made to appear in slow motion when projected on the screen at the standard projection speed, and by using a slower filming speed, action appears to take place much more quickly on the screen.

If your cine camera is fitted with a single frame shot facility you can make time lapse sequences very easily indeed. These are the sequences which you sometimes see in nature films where a flower appears to open out from a tiny bud to a full-blown bloom in two or three seconds. This is achieved by exposing a single frame every ten seconds or so during the entire time that it takes for the flower to open. This calls for a lot of patience because it can mean sitting around for several hours pressing the single shot cable release once every ten seconds. But several of the more advanced movie cameras available today have attachments which will do this automatically. You merely attach the device to your cine camera and set a control to however many seconds you want to elapse between exposures and switch the machine on. From that point until you switch it off the time lapse attachment will operate the camera shutter once every time the mechanism is activated. So you can leave the camera to get on with the filming by itself for as long as you like.

One very interesting time lapse sequence that I saw on television recently was a whole day, from sunrise to sunset, which appeared to take place in the space of about two minutes. The effect was quite startling; clouds went scudding across the sky at breakneck speed, and the sun was seen visibly to move in an arc across the sky. Another time lapse sequence that proved very interesting was of a train journey between London and Edinburgh which appeared to take place at something well over the speed of sound!

Obviously when you are taking a time lapse sequence of this sort, you must have your movie camera rigidly mounted on a tripod, because the slightest movement from a fixed position will show up in the film as a wavering movement.

Time lapse sequences are extensively used in scientific movie making, especially in the field of biology, but they can be just as spectacular in an amateur home movie. But just as with any other sequence which relies on the unusual for its effect, be careful not to overdo it. Even if your cine camera does not have the facility for taking single frame exposures, you can, if you are careful, achieve a time lapse sequence. You do this by simply pressing the shutter control and releasing it immediately so that the camera shoots only one or two frames. However, this takes quite a lot of practice to avoid jarring the camera and causing it to move, with the result that the sequence would jump about on the screen and would tend to be blurred. As with pan and zoom shots, it is as well to begin a time lapse sequence with the camera held on the object for a few seconds and to finish with another two or three second hold filmed at the normal running speed of your camera.

Since time lapse photography is a specialised field, I can cover it only very briefly in this book. If you would like to know more about it you will find the information in some of the books listed in the bibliography at the end of this book.

Using Filters

In addition to the filter built into your Super 8 camera to enable you to shoot in daylight with the basic artificial light type Super 8 film, there is a whole range of other filters available which you can use to create effects in your movies. For practical amateur work in colour these filters can be divided into five types: skylight filters, ultra-violet absorbing filters, haze filters, colour temperature correction filters, and polarising filters. You will not, of course, need all of these filters but a small selection can provide you with a considerable amount of extra control in your movie making. Let us take a look at each type in turn.

Skylight, UV, and haze filters

To a certain extent, these three filters all do the same basic job. They are designed to reduce excess blueness in shadows when you are filming on a bright sunny day and the shadows are lit by blue skylight. Of the three types, the skylight filter is the most effective and therefore the most useful. It has a secondary use on rainy days or dull, overcast days when it adds a little bit of warmth to the subject because it is very slightly pink in colour. If you want a filter which removes excess blueness from shadows, choose the skylight filter.

The UV filter also tends to counteract excess blueness in the shadows lit by skylight, but since it is slightly yellow in colour it can produce a rather strange yellowish sky when there is heavy cloud cover.

The haze filter is something of a misnomer since it does not, as its name would seem to imply, cut through haze to clear the distance in long landscape shots. In fact the haze filter is usually colourless and seems to have very little effect at all.

Colour temperature correction filters

You will probably have noticed that sunlight in the early morning and late evening is very much redder than it is at mid-day. In fact the colour of sunlight is changing constantly throughout the day; this colour is known as colour temperature and can be defined precisely in scientific terms.

Colour films are balanced for one specific colour temperature; in the case of Super 8 movie films it is the colour temperature of artificial light and a conversion filter enables the film to be used in daylight. Now since daylight varies in colour from early morning, through noon to sunset and the conversion filter will only adapt the film with any degree of accuracy to the colour temperature of daylight at noon, if you want to film before about ten o'clock in the morning or after two or three o'clock in the afternoon during the summer, the results on your film will tend to get progressively warmer or more orange the earlier or later you shoot.

You can counteract this by using colour temperature correction filters which are available in two basic colours: reddish and bluish; and usually in four strengths; $1\frac{1}{2}$, 3, 6, and 12. These figures are units called decamireds, the meaning of which we need not go into here.

For early and late filming you would use a bluish filter of about $1\frac{1}{2}$ or 3 decamireds and if you were filming totally in shadow, lit only by deep blue skylight, you would use a reddish filter of about 3 decamireds, or possibly 6. However, my basic advice on filters is not to use them unless you absolutely have to because they nearly always adversely affect the performance of the camera lens by causing a loss of contrast due to the slight amount of flare that they can introduce. The only time to use filters of this type is if you find that a lot of film that you shoot has a pronounced reddish or bluish cast when projected. Then buy a filter to correct this and use it only in the lighting conditions which have produced the cast on your film.

Polarising filter

This, in my opinion, is by far the most useful filter of all. It works on the same principle as Polaroid sunglasses and cuts out unwanted reflections in glass and other non-metallic objects. But more than this, it can darken the blue of the sky in a picture without altering any of the other colours in the shot. This in turn gives you a certain amount of control over the brightness and contrast of your picture.

All filters with the exception of the skylight, UV and haze filters reduce the amount of light entering the camera lens and therefore the exposure has to be increased to compensate for this. However, with modern automatic exposure control systems in most Super 8 cine cameras, this need not worry you because the compensation is applied automatically.

6 Editing your movie

Good editing is just as important to a successful movie as good camera work, because it is at this stage that the individual filmed sequences are put together into a smooth-running whole. Unfortunately, because it appears, on the face of it, to be a somewhat irksome task, editing is often neglected to the point where it never gets done at all. Yet if it is done properly, editing need not be in the least an unpleasant task and can, in fact, play as big a part in the overall fun of movie making as shooting the film in the first place.

How much time you spend on editing depends entirely on how much work you want to do on the film. Always remember, the best editing is that which is done in the camera at the time of shooting. It is also the least expensive since that way you do not waste expensive film.

When your movie film comes back from the processing laboratory it is in a single fifty foot length, ready spooled for projecting. If you have been on holiday, it is a fair assumption that you will have shot several cartridges of film during the week or fortnight you were away, especially if you spent the holiday somewhere which was new to you. So after processing you will have, perhaps, half a dozen small spools of film and when you want to project them you will have to do so one spool at a time and the whole show becomes a series of isolated pieces, each of rather less than four minutes duration. And that is not going to impress anyone. Simply joining all the individual spools together to form one continuous movie is not going to improve things very much. In fact the only thing you are going to do is save yourself the bother of having to re-thread the projector every three or four minutes.

To make your film presentation more acceptable, more interesting, more entertaining, and generally more professional, you must rearrange some of the sequences that you have shot while on holiday so that the film holds together and tells some sort of story, which is basically what we are trying to do. But before discussing the methods of editing we must look at the mechanical side of the process and the equipment needed to do the job. The technique of editing a movie is very simple

Tape splicer and tapes for easy splicing

indeed. It consists of merely cutting the film into individual sequences and joining them together in a logical progression. So the equipment that you need, in its most basic form, is something to cut the film with and something to join it together again. You will also need some means of viewing the film so that you can stop it at any individual frame.

Splicers

The points at which individual pieces of film are joined together are called splices and the device which makes the cuts in the pieces of film to enable them to be joined together is called a splicer.

Splicing lengths of film together used to be a fiddly, messy job requiring bottles of film cement, fairly expensive splicers and some means of scraping the emulsion off the surface of the film to allow the cement to adhere to the base and hold the two lengths of film firmly together. Fortunately, splicing film has become a great deal easier and less messy in recent years, thanks to the introduction of an alternative system which makes use of transparent self-adhesive strips which join the two lengths of film together. And, even better, these new style splicers are only a fraction of the cost of the older type. But if you prefer to use cement for splicing, there are now semi-automatic cement splicers available which do make the job rather easier. Really, the cost angle is a bit of a swings and roundabouts affair; the initial cost of a cement type splicer is higher than that of a tape splicer, but the cement is far cheaper than the special transparent splicing tape which you use with a tape splicer.

In addition to the splicer you will need either a bottle of film cement or a packet of self-adhesive splicing tapes. These tapes are normally pre-cut to the correct length.

Viewers

Most film viewers available on the amateur market consist of a small viewing screen on which the film is projected and a pair of reel holders with geared hand wheels, one on either side of the viewing screen. The whole set-up is, in many ways, rather like a miniature movie projector but without an electric motor to drive it. The whole set-up is sometimes called a film editor, though I think that viewer is probably the better description.

The viewer operates on the very simple principle that as the film passes through an illuminated gate, a rotating prism picks up one frame at a time and diverts it through a short focal length projecting lens on to a mirror and then to the viewing screen. A focus control enables you to produce a sharp image on the screen and a framing control allows you to adjust the image so that you see just a single frame on the screen rather than two halves of adjacent frames. If you are offered a viewer without these two basic controls, reject it.

To operate the machine, you feed the film through the gate, switch on the lamp, and turn one or other of the geared hand wheels on the reel holders. This then transports the film in a forward or backward direction and enables you to stop at any particular frame, which means that your editing can be really accurate. Many of these viewers have a small lever which enables you to make a mark on the edge of the film alongside the particular frame where you want to cut the film.

Raynox RS-3000 editing set-up

When you choose a viewer pay particular attention to the area around the gate where the film is fed through, because some of the very cheap models are not too well made and have small rough edges left which can cause scratching on the film. Also check the brightness and sharpness of the image on the viewing screen. The best way to do this is to take along a spool of your own film when you go to the shop so that you can compare one viewer with another. One other important point you should look for when buying a viewer is that the reel holders are capable of holding at least a 400 foot reel, and preferably an even larger one; you never know when you may want to make a feature length movie.

To begin with, you will probably have laid out quite a lot of money on your cine equipment: a camera, a projector, a screen, maybe a tripod, and most of all on film. So you may be a little hesitant about spending another thirty pounds or so on a viewer. It is possible to use a projector as a viewer when you are editing, if you are prepared to put up with a certain amount of inconvenience. For instance, it is not usually possible to stop a projector on a particular frame, so you can only mark the approximate area and you will have to examine the frames closely with a magnifier to find the particular frame which you want to cut. However, even with this slight inconvenience, editing a film with the aid of a projector is far better than not editing it at all. One problem you may run into, though, in using a projector for editing purposes, is that the continual switching on and off of the lamp may shorten its life considerably. And projector lamps are not cheap.

Film Hanger

The only other piece of equipment needed for editing movies is some means of holding the individual pieces of film in the correct order once they have been cut, so that you can select any one to insert in the film when you want it. But this piece of equipment – it is usually called a film hanger – is one which you can very easily make for yourself.

In its simplest form, a film hanger need consist only of a piece of string stretched between two convenient points and with a dozen or so spring clip clothes pegs to suspend the pieces of film. If you want to make something a little more elaborate than this you can glue spring clip clothes pegs to a length of wood and use this in the same way. As you hang up each piece of film, clip a small paper label with it to identify the scene so that you can find any particular sequence very quickly.

One other final piece of equipment is a pair of very fine, soft cotton gloves which you should always wear when handling film for editing purposes to avoid leaving greasy fingermarks on the delicate surface of the film. Even though you may think your hands are perfectly clean and dry, you will find that they still leave traces of grease behind on the film and these can ruin an otherwise perfect movie.

Splicing

As I have already mentioned, there are two basic types of splicer for amateur use, the cement type and the tape type. Which you choose is largely a matter of personal preference; I personally favour the more simple tape splicer since it is much easier for the beginner to handle. However, since I can deal with both types fairly quickly, I shall do so.

Splicing with cement

A cement splicer consists essentially of two metal clamps, one on the left and one on the right, each intended to hold one of the lengths of film you want to join together.

The first step is to place the two pieces of film, emulsion (dull) side up, into their appropriate clamping plates, making sure that the film perforations are accurately fitted on the special register pins incorporated in the clamps. Leave a short length of the film – about two frames long – sticking out from each of the clamps so that they overlap slightly. Next, close the clamps; this automatically trims off the ends of the film square. You must now swing one of the clamps up and out of the way while you scrape the emulsion off the other piece of film with a razor blade or with a special built-in scraper which is incorporated into many splicers. Brush all traces of the scraped emulsion away from the film, then you must apply the cement, which is a kind of cellulose solvent, with a brush or a glass rod supplied with the bottle of cement, and swing the other clamp back down so that the second piece of film is brought into contact with the cemented piece. Leave the two pieces of film in contact while the cement sets; about twenty to thirty seconds. Finally, remove the film from the splicer and tug the two halves to make sure that the splice has really taken. This is an essential part of the operation because if the splice is poorly-made the film will come apart the first time you try to project it.

Splicing with tape

The tape splicer is a much simpler device than the cement one and usually consists of a moulded plastic base with registration pins to locate the film perforations, and a hinged plastic top which contains a sharp cutting knife. The big advantage is that you do not need to scrape the film as with cement splicing and the whole operation is a dry one.

First of all, place one piece of film in the splicer, emulsion side up, and cut it by bringing down the hinged piece containing the knife. Then do the same with the other piece of film, bringing it in from the other side of the splicer, of course. Next, butt the two pieces of film together – again using the registration pins in the splicer – and put a short length of splicing tape over the join. This splicing tape has perforations which correspond with those in the film, so you can align the tape on the registration pins, too. Then turn the film over and repeat the operation on the other side. That is all there is to it.

Tape splicing is a very tough way of joining film; it is much more convenient; it is much less messy; and it is certainly much easier for the beginner to master quickly. All of which explains why I recommend it rather than the cement splice.

Whichever method of splicing you decide to use, it is well worth prac-
tising on a few bits of old scrap film before you try to edit a full movie.
Then you can get down to the exciting job of putting together your first
movie.

Making the First Cuts

The first task when you begin to edit any movie is to cut the individual
spools of film into separate sequences; even if you eventually intend any
two sequences to follow each other in the same order, you should
separate them at this stage.

Splicing with tape – see text

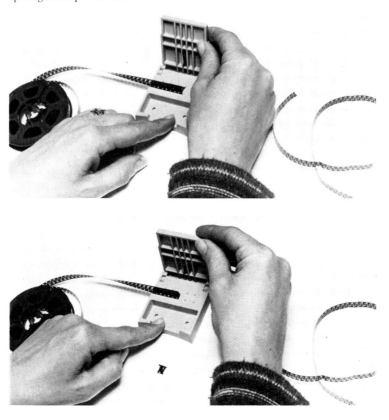

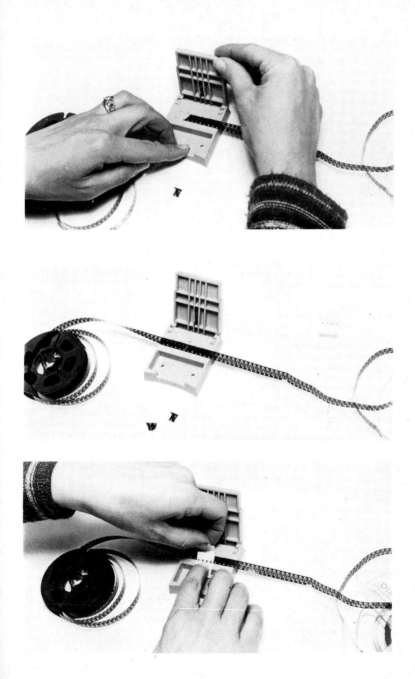

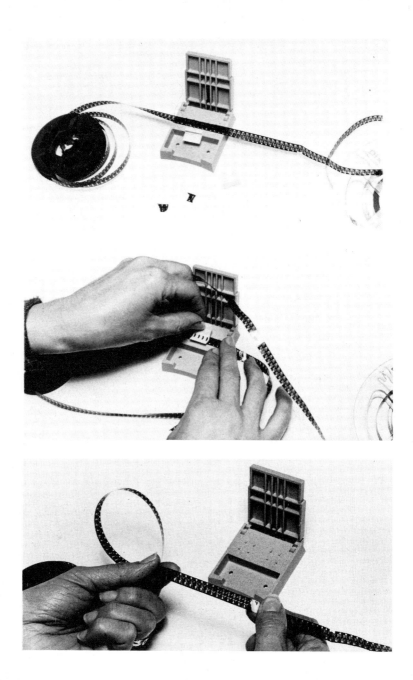

Run each individual fifty foot spool of film through your viewer and with the marking lever mark the beginning of each sequence. When the full fifty feet have been through the viewer cut the film into its separate scenes, hanging each one on the clothes peg film hanger described earlier.

When all the films are cut into individual sequences, sort them into the order in which you want them to appear in the finished movie before splicing them all together in this order. At this stage you still have the full footage which you shot in the camera for every scene, and the next stage is to get rid of the pieces of film which you wish to scrap for one reason or another. This is called making a rough cut.

The rough cut

Even though you are going to have to go through your film again after making a rough cut, it is always advisable to carry out this important first stage once you have joined all the different sequences together in the order in which you want them to appear.

Before you go back to the editing bench to start cutting the film, run it through your projector in its entire form just to see what the general effect is. Have by your side a pad of paper and a pencil so that you can jot down any sequences which you feel should be removed totally or relocated in the final version.

Obviously, the first pieces of film to go are those which are out of focus, wrongly exposed, or where the subject is tilted in the frame. Having noted these down, re-run the film in the projector and this time make a note of the best sequences which are left in the film, especially if you have shot from more than one angle for a particular scene.

Now it is back to the editing bench to remove all the unwanted pieces of film. Throw away the technically bad pieces straight away, for they can have no further use, but save the other shots which you have edited out because they may come in useful later for brief cutaway shots or even for use in a different movie.

Run the film through the projector yet again and see if there are any other changes of sequence you wish to make, and make a note of any scenes which you feel may be improved by being shorter. When you have done this you can begin to edit these scenes down using the splicer and the bench viewer until you get the film to the stage where you are feeling fairly happy with it.

One tip worth remembering is to try not to work on the film as a whole; instead, work on each individual scene separately so that you can try to work out your timing for each scene as accurately as possible. However, at this stage, if you have any doubts at all about the length of a scene, leave it rather too long than too short; you can always cut a little more out of it later.

When you have carried out this first editing put the film back through the projector again and look at it really critically. By now, all the scenes should be in their final order and of approximately the right length. Now you should be looking for slight errors in timing. In other words, scenes which are just a little longer than they should be and which might be improved by cutting one or two seconds or even less. Make notes while you project the film and go through the whole movie again if you have any doubts in your mind about how you want to make your final edit.

Mistakes and how to correct them

When you are editing your first few movies it is almost inevitable that you will make the odd mistake – cutting a scene too short, cutting a scene that you did not intend to cut at all, or, more seriously, finding that you are jumping from one scene to another with no logical link. Once you have edited a few films and gained a little experience, these mistakes will not worry you unduly, but here are a few tips which can perhaps help you to save the day in your earlier efforts.

To take the simplest example: if you find that you have cut a scene too short or cut a piece of film accidentally, and you are using the tape splicing method where the two pieces of film are butt-jointed together, you can simply re-join them with an additional splice and in most cases, no-one will be any the wiser. However, if you are using a cement splicer you will lose at least one frame every time you make a splice, and probably as many as four frames. Now obviously, when this is projected it is going to lead to a jump in the action at the point where you made the mistake. This is where some of those additional shots which you cut out in the original editing can come in useful as cutaways.

Cutaways are simply very short sequences lasting at the most a second or so, which can be inserted between two pieces of film showing a single sequence. Assume, for example, that you have been filming a motor race and you accidentally cut a sequence where a car is speeding past you at 120 mph or so. Even if you only lose four frames of the sequence by accidentally cutting it in the wrong place, the car will have moved several yards further forward during that short space of time. Therefore, if you simply stick the film back together again the car will appear to leap physically several yards forward and will look most strange on the screen.

If at some other point in the race you have shot a short sequence of some of the spectators eating hamburgers, drinking bottles of beer or cups of coffee, which in your original editing you decided to leave out of the film, you can insert a few frames between the two sequences of the car travelling past you. This will have the effect of showing the car approaching, cutting away to the reaction on the spectators' faces, then back to the car as it moves past you. In fact doing this would probably improve the whole of that particular scene. If you have only lost, say, four frames due to your accidental cutting, you will probably need to cut a little more out of the original sequence because just inserting four frames of the cutaway to cover the accident will amount to rather less than a quarter of a second on the screen, and this is obviously far too short for even the simplest cutaway. As a general rule, I would advise never going below half a second, and even that is cutting things a little fine. This means that you will probably have to cut out a few more frames from the original sequence. Since you know the speed at which the film passes through the camera – 18 frames per second – it is a simple matter to count how many frames to remove to allow for a cutaway of a given length. For example, if you want a half-second cutaway, this will need nine frames of the cutaway scene. So if you lost four due to your accidental cut you will need to remove another five from the original sequence to make up the total number of frames which are being replaced by the cutaway.

You can use this cutaway technique very successfully to link together two sequences which would otherwise tend to make the film appear disjointed. The principle is exactly the same. And if you do not have a suitable cutaway sequence, you can always shoot one later as long as you remember that it must do the job of linking the other two sequences together.

Final adjustments

By now you should have your movie into pretty well its final form, and all that remains to be done is to project it on to the screen two or three more times just to make sure that you are quite happy with it. If you still feel that there are one or two sequences that could be tightened up slightly, do not be afraid to cut them yet again. The whole movie will only gain from this extra fine cutting.

Do not be afraid to cut

I suppose it must be something to do with human nature that having spent quite a lot of time – and money – in shooting movie film during your holiday it goes rather against the grain to cut a lot of it out in the final version which you will show on the screen. But this, after all, is rather a negative way of looking at it; try thinking positively instead. Remember that the tighter and more closely knit the final version of the film is, the more impact it will have on your audience. The trick is to leave the audience wanting more.

Perhaps the best example of this can be seen every evening on independent television. Commercials (advertising films) are usually either fifteen, thirty, or sixty seconds in length; the vast majority are either fifteen or thirty seconds. Yet into that short space of time the advertiser (or rather the advertiser's film director) has to tell the story of his product, put over the benefits of that product, and persuade us to go out and buy the product. Despite what the sceptics may believe – or say they believe – the best commercials do these three jobs very effectively indeed. So next time the commercials come on to your small screen, do not ignore them, or even try to ignore them; study them instead, for these short advertising films really are masterpieces of tight editing and you can learn a lot from them.

Yet even movies which will ultimately be as short as television commercials are often edited down from a great deal more original footage, because there is one basic philosophy in editing: it is always easier to edit footage which contains a large number of different sequences and different types of long, medium and close-up shot than it is to edit a film which has been tightly shot in the first place. Unless, of course, you shot your film tightly because that is the way you had planned it in your mind before you even started to shoot, in which case my remark at the beginning of this chapter that the best editing is done in the camera holds true. But despite this basic thought, I would always recommend that, when in doubt, shoot more rather than less, and edit the film later when you have had a chance to assemble the individual sequences into some sort of order.

One final thought on editing which should, in fact, be the most obvious and foremost principle. When you have assembled your film from the individual sequences, make sure that the events which are being shown on the screen appear to happen in a natural, logical order. In other words, make your movie appear real. If there is any sequence in there which, on your final scrutiny, appears to be out of place, then either re-arrange the movie with this sequence in a different position or lose the sequence altogether. If you do not, it will ruin the film because to the audience it will simply make the whole movie unbelievable, and that is possibly the worst thing that can happen to all that carefully shot, carefully edited footage which you have so painstakingly put together.

7 Adding sound

While it has always been possible for the amateur movie maker to make his films with sound, it has, until comparatively recently, been a rather difficult process involving the use of a tape recorder linked to, and synchronised with, the movie camera. This had two basic disadvantages: in the first place it was rather large and cumbersome, and in the second, it was very expensive. But that was not the end of the story. Once the film had been shot in the camera, and the sound recorded on the tape recorder, you had to set up your projector and tape recorder in synchronisation each time you showed your film, and this was notoriously difficult; the problem was that the synchronisation kept varying.

An alternative system called sound striping involves re-recording the sound from your tape recorder on to a strip of what is, basically, recording tape attached to the side of the film. This has an advantage in that once the system is synchronised it remains so.

However, the dream of many home movie enthusiasts — and the companies which manufacture cine cameras and equipment — was to have a compact single machine capable of shooting the film and recording the sound simultaneously, and in synchronisation. This dream has now been realised. Modern sound movies are well within the scope of anyone, and involve very little more than shooting silent movies.

The introduction of this type of sound camera has been one of the major developments in amateur movie making in recent years, and is typified by the Kodak Ektasound system.

Making sound movies is not very different from making silent movies, except that you have to take into consideration the sound that is going on around you as well as the visible movement, and you must learn the additional techniques of handling and placing a microphone to achieve the best possible results.

Sound at its Simplest

If you merely want to record the sound of what is happening in the action of your movie, additional technique is as simple as pointing the

Kodak Ektasound 160 camera

microphone in the same general direction as the camera lens. In fact, many sound cameras have the microphone mounted on a boom on top of the camera to enable you to do this in the easiest possible way. Added to this, most modern Super 8 sound cameras are fitted with an electronic device called Automatic Gain Control or AGC which is, in effect, the sound equivalent of the automatic exposure control built into the camera for making sure that you expose your films correctly.

What AGC does, in fact, is to adjust automatically the amplifier which is built into the camera to record the sound on the special Super 8 sound film and so maintain a uniform level of recorded sound.

In the section on automatic exposure control, I pointed out that there are certain situations where the automatic control does not give the best possible exposure to your film, such as when a scene is predominantly light or predominantly dark. The same thing applies to the automatic gain control in a sound camera.

Basically, AGC adjusts the volume of the recorded sound to suit the loudest signal which is received by the microphone. This, of course, is fine, as long as the loudest signal received by the microphone is the one that you want to record. However, it may be that there is an unwanted sound while you are filming which may be louder than the sound that you *do* want, and the AGC system in the camera will base the recording level on this rather than on the sound that you want. A typical example is an aircraft flying overhead just at the moment when you wish to record a conversation between two people. So check that there are no loud, unwanted sounds before you start filming. Some cameras have gone part way towards solving this problem by supplying an additional microphone socket with reduced sensitivity. When the microphone is plugged into this socket the effect of background noise is reduced.

Going One Better

While the simple point and shoot method of using the microphone will probably satisfy you for your first few cartridges of sound film, it is unlikely to do so for very much longer, especially if you are at all self-critical. Fortunately, though, it does not take much more effort to produce very good sound movies than it does to produce mediocre ones.

Elmo 350 SL sound camera with microphone on attached boom

And the key to better sound movies lies in using the microphone correctly.

Using the microphone

Always remember that the recording track on your Super 8 sound film can only record what the microphone feeds to it. If the microphone picks up a strong signal you will get a good recording, but if the signal picked up is weak and distorted, the recording likewise will be weak and distorted. And if there is any background noise from the camera drive mechanism, the microphone will pick that up too and add it to the film sound track.

So, the first thing to do to improve the quality of sound movies is to get the microphone away from the camera so that it does not pick up the sound of the camera itself; separate the microphone and the camera by as much as you conveniently can. Unfortunately, this is often easier said than done and you may find that you need the help of an assistant to look after the microphone while you concentrate on the filming.

Ideally, the microphone should be between one and five feet from the sound you want to record. At these distances you are likely to pick up a strong signal from your subject and minimise background noise from further away. The simplest way to get your microphone into the best position for recording is to mount it on a boom – a long length of metal tubing or dowel rod – which enables you or your assistant to hold the microphone in the best position for recording. For most situations, holding the microphone above and slightly in front of your subject gives the best results. If you are filming indoors it is usually possible to suspend the microphone in this position by hanging it on a piece of string from the ceiling.

The microphones supplied with most amateur movie cameras are of lightweight plastic construction and can be easily secured to the boom or any other suitable object with cellulose tape. Obviously, it does not look very professional, or even competent, to have the microphone in the picture, so take a little time and trouble to ensure that the microphone is out of frame. If you find that you cannot do this for some reason – maybe you are shooting a long shot and cannot get the microphone sufficiently close to your subject without it being in frame – you can often disguise it fairly easily by hiding it behind another object in the picture. For example, if it is an indoor shot you may be able to position the microphone behind an ornament or a table lamp so that it cannot be seen from the camera position. However, if you do this be sure to disguise the cable from the microphone as well.

If you find that you do have to conceal the microphone within the

The microphone can be placed inside the camera case while filming to cut background noise from the camera

frame while you shoot your sound movie, try to avoid placing it on a hard surface such as direct on a table, because this can act as a sounding board and can cause the sound picked up by the microphone to be distorted and the quality of the sound on your movie will therefore suffer. A few pieces of thick polythene foam or felt carried in your camera bag can be used to rest the microphone on in such cases.

One thing you must try not to do at all costs is to hand-hold the microphone, because the casing of the microphone will pick up the slightest movement of your fingers, and even the cable rubbing against your clothing will be transmitted on to the recording as a highly magnified rustle or crackle which will completely ruin the sound track of the film. If you really do not have any alternative but to hand hold the mike, hold it firmly and avoid changing your grip or twisting and bending the cable. In this way you can minimise the stray mechanical noises picked up on the recording.

Sound Filming Indoors

Try to remember that all surfaces reflect sound to some degree or other, but that those which do so most effectively are hard smooth surfaces, such as furniture, doors, windows, and so on, while those which reflect sound the least are curtains, soft furnishing fabrics, carpets, and the like. To some extent this will govern where you shoot your sound movie. If you have the choice, you will obviously try to avoid filming in a kitchen, which is full of hard reflective surfaces, and has few, if any, soft, absorbent ones. The same would apply to the bathroom, but not to such a degree. But obviously, if a scene you are shooting requires to be shot in a kitchen or bathroom you will have to do so. But in this case you can help to solve the problem by hanging thick curtains or old blankets behind the camera to give at least some degree of absorbency.

The ideal place to film your indoor sequences would be a living room with thick wall to wall carpeting, soft padded furniture and thick heavy curtains. All these help to absorb and deaden sound so that the sound picked up by the microphone is relatively unaffected by reflections and other distortions.

Microphones are often considerably more sensitive than the human ear, so be careful that there are no radios, record players, or television sets switched on in other parts of the house. While you may not notice these at the time, it is quite likely that the microphone will pick up sounds from them and will record them as background noise on the recording of your sound movie.

Shooting Outdoors

You should have less problems with reflected and distorted sounds outdoors because there are fewer hard smooth surfaces to reflect and distort the sound. But even so, take as many precautions as you can and try to use the microphone in situations where there are wide open spaces or trees and bushes rather than rocks. One thing that you may have trouble with when shooting sound movies outdoors is wind noise. Even a slight breeze blowing across the microphone will record rather like a muffled roar that sounds more like a waterfall or a raging torrent than a slight breeze. The same thing applies when you are recording in fairly heavy rain which tends to sound like the snaps, crackles and pops of the well-known breakfast cereal rather than falling water.

Many microphones for sound movie use are supplied complete with a protective tube which fits over the head of the microphone. This is made from a porous plastic material which is designed to let sound through while minimising the noise caused by wind or rain. If your microphone does not have such a tube you can often make do by wrapping a handkerchief around it.

Certain types of sound outdoors, however, are difficult *not* to record well. If I may use my well-tried example of filming a motor race again; the sound the cars make is so loud and so characteristic that it is difficult for them not to sound like racing cars. And, incidentally, this is one of the particular cases where sound really does add a lot to a film: whoever heard of silent racing cars?

Using Other Microphones

The type of microphone supplied with most amateur sound movie cameras is a rather simple and inexpensive device; consequently it is rather limited in its application and you can do wonders for your sound movies simply by swapping it for a better quality microphone. Provided, of course, that its electrical characteristics match the requirements of the camera.

Usually the type of microphone provided with the camera as standard is known as an omnidirectional type. This means that it picks up sound from all directions. While this type of microphone does have its uses, for many types of filming it is relatively unsuitable because you may want to record sounds from one direction only.

The other main type of microphone which is used in amateur movie making is the directional or cardioid type. This, as its name implies, has a heart-shaped pickup pattern taking in sounds from the front and, to a lesser extent, from the sides, but ignoring sounds from directly behind it. This type of microphone can be extremely useful in situations where background noise is causing trouble. It is particularly useful for recording a voice-over type of commentary rather than dialogue between characters in the movie. In fact, for this latter type of conversation the omnidirectional microphone is a much safer bet.

The electrical characteristics that I mentioned earlier are the impedance and voltage output of the microphone. In practically every case, the microphone suitable for Super 8 sound movies is low impedance and with a voltage output of about six milli-volts. Fortunately, this is the same sort of specification as microphones used for most cassette and reel-to-reel tape recorders, so any of the better quality microphones which are suitable for tape recorders will generally be suitable for your sound camera, too. But to be sure, check with the instructional manual supplied with your camera, and if you are in any doubt at all, check with the shop assistant when you buy your new microphone.

An increasing number of photographic dealers also sell high fidelity sound equipment, so you should be able to buy your new microphone from any one of these dealers.

Sound quality

Probably the most important thing that buying a better microphone will do for your movies is give you improved sound quality. But only to a certain extent. Sound quality is governed primarily by the speed at which the magnetic recording stripe on the side of the film passes the recording head in the camera; the faster it moves past the head, the better the quality of the sound will be. Therefore, if you want to make a significant improvement in the quality of the sound on your films, you will have to film at a higher speed than the standard 18 frames per second.

If both your camera and your projector have the facility for a film speed of 24 fps, I would advise you to use them because the increase in recorded quality of sound you will get with this small increase in filming speed will be quite noticeable. It will mean, of course, that you use the film more quickly, and therefore your movie will cost you more in cash terms, but if quality is important to you, then it will be well worth it. Indeed, if you are shooting a sequence which involves music, you are likely to be most disappointed with the results if you shoot at 18 fps because the range of tones produced by a group of instruments – or even a single instrument – is far greater than that produced by the human voice, and while a slow speed may be perfectly adequate for dialogue, it is unlikely to be so for recording music.

A Problem

Nothing can bring as many advantages and improvements to home movies that simple sound has done without bringing with it at least one problem. And Super 8 sound movies are no exception. The problem is splicing and editing your sound films.

While the techniques of editing silent Super 8 movies are fairly straightforward, they are complicated when you use sound by the fact that pictures and their associated sound track are not side by side. They are, in fact, separated by eighteen frames; the sound for a particular frame is recorded eighteen frames in front of the picture, which corresponds to a time difference of one second. Obviously if you attempt to edit your film in the normal way, you are going to cut the wrong piece of sound track for the picture you are looking at. However, there is a way round this problem; in fact, there are two ways.

In the first place you can plan your movie very carefully before you start to shoot it and shoot all the sequences in their correct order and for their correct length. But this, as you will have realised by now, is not as easy as it sounds. The second solution to the problem is to leave one or two seconds silent at the beginning and end of each scene. This allows

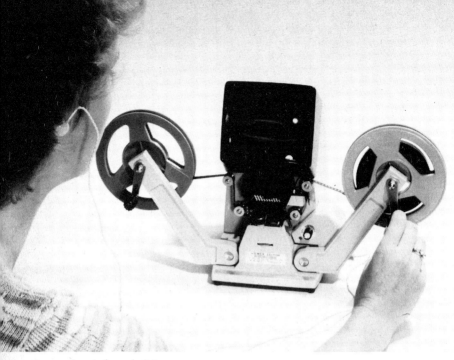

A typical sound editing set-up

you enough leeway to cut at the beginning or end of each sequence without cutting into recorded sound track.

Incidentally, if you splice your sound films using the tape type of splicer, a tip worth remembering is to trim about a sixteenth of an inch from the edge of the tape opposite the perforations. If you do not do this the tape will cover the sound track and cause a sudden lowering of volume of sound as it passes the sound head. This small amount trimmed off the tape, however, is sufficient to clear the sound track and leave the volume unaltered.

Changing a Recording

Many of the special projectors for showing Super 8 sound films have the facility for recording sound as well as for replaying it: they are, in effect, rather like small tape recorders. This means that if you are not happy with the sound track of a particular sequence on your film, or if you want to record background music for a moody shot you can do so quite simply.

Some sound projectors incorporate recording facilities for recording after filming. Elmo ST12001

This sort of thing can be quite effective if it is used properly. For example, in the Stanley Kubrick film '2001 – A Space Odyssey', Strauss' Blue Danube waltz was recorded as background music to a sequence where a space ship was manoeuvring to dock at a satellite space station and the effect was most appropriate.

The introduction of a simple system of making sound movies has widened the horizons of the amateur cine photographer beyond his wildest dreams of ten years or so ago. With a lot of practice, patience and determination, it is possible to produce really professional quality films that will do what all good films should do: leave your audience wanting more.

8 Showing your movies

The ultimate reason for buying a cine camera and making your own movies is to show them to your family and friends. To do this you need a projector, a screen, and a room which can be darkened so that your audience can view the film to its best advantage. These are the basic necessities for showing your home movies. By spending a little time and thought on the way in which you show your films you can make the whole presentation far more professional. And that generally means that it will be more enjoyable, more interesting, and more entertaining for your audience. First, however, let us have a look at the equipment you need for showing your films.

The Projector

With the sole exception of your movie camera, your cine projector is the most important piece of equipment that you are likely to buy for your hobby of movie photography, and there is just as much variety in projectors on the market as there is in cameras. So what do you look for?

The first and most important generalisation is to buy a projector that will do justice to the quality of the films produced by your movie camera. In other words, if you have spent a lot of money buying a really first class movie camera, do not buy a cheap projector and expect it to do full justice to the results from that camera; you will need to buy an expensive projector to do justice to your films. But by the same token, if you have bought a simple, fixed focus movie camera, you will be wasting your money by buying an expensive, advanced projector to show your films.

Projectors start in price at about £30 – much the same sort of price that movie cameras start at – and for this amount of money you would get a basic machine with a fixed focal length lens, probably just one projection speed, and rewind facilities. Starting at around £50 you will be able to buy a somewhat better projector, probably with an extra projection speed and the facility for reverse projection, and possibly with a

Agfa Movector 2000 – an excellent mid-priced projector

zoom lens. Projectors in this sort of price range are perfectly adequate for films produced on simple cameras, including those in the lower price range which have non-focusing zoom lenses. If your camera is somewhat better than this, you will need to spend a bit more on your projector; for about £80 to £100 you can buy a very good projector with forward and reverse running, at least two speeds, and a good quality zoom lens, together with, of course, rewind facilities. In my opinion, a particularly good buy in this price range is the Agfa Movector 2000 which currently sells for just under £90.

Projectors costing over £100 are really only worth investing in if you have a first class, almost professional quality Super 8 movie camera. These projectors have extra facilities which cheaper models do not have,

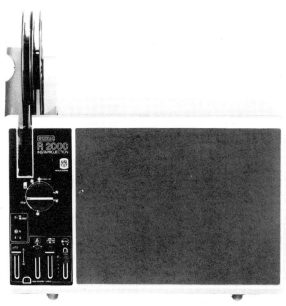

Eumig R2000 table-top projector

such as extra speeds and the facility for instant reverse. Some may take larger spools than the less expensive projectors, although most of these will take up to 400 foot reels, which is sufficient for most purposes.

One particularly interesting projector which has recently appeared on the market is the Eumig R2000, which is a self-contained table top machine giving a picture about the same size as, and rather like in character, a television picture. The advantage of this machine, of course, is that it needs no separate screen and can be set up virtually anywhere. But the projected picture is rather on the small size.

If you have progressed into sound movies your choice of projectors is fairly wide again, but you will naturally have to pay more for the projector because it has the extra facility of sound. A particularly interesting and unusual sound projector is the Kodak Ektasound which, like the Eumig silent projector, is a completely new concept in movie projectors. In fact it looks more like a tape recorder than a projector, with the reels side by side and the optical system incorporating a mirror which turns the image through ninety degrees. The advantage of this design is that it can be stood on a bookshelf with its back right against the wall and therefore needs very little space in which to operate.

Many projectors have the facility to accept both Super 8 and the old Standard 8 movie films. If you have, perhaps, been involved with home movies for some time and have a stock of Standard 8 films, it is worth while buying one of these dual standard projectors, but if you are just starting out on the hobby you will find that you will almost certainly never use the projector in its Standard 8 mode, therefore there seems little point in spending extra money on a facility that you may never use.

The projector lens

Projectors at the cheaper end of the price range are normally fitted with a lens of fixed focal length. With this type of projector, if you want to alter the size of the picture on the screen you must change the distance between the projector and the screen. However, it is now possible to buy a reasonably inexpensive projector fitted with a zoom lens – most of the more expensive projectors are fitted with zoom lenses as standard anyway – the advantage that this has is that you can alter the image size on the screen by simply changing the setting of the zoom lens, leaving the projector in the most convenient position in the room.

One word of warning: if you are thinking of buying a projector in the lower price range fitted with a zoom lens, check the quality of the picture by seeing a length of film – preferably your own – projected before you buy the projector, because some of the cheaper zoom lenses can give poor definition, especially round the edges of the picture, and can introduce aberrations or distortions in the picture. Zoom lenses on more expensive projectors, however, should not suffer from this shortcoming.

Projectors from the medium price range and up usually have at least two running speeds and these are normally 18 and 24 frames per second – the two most commonly used filming speeds. 18 fps is, of course, the standard for silent movies and 24 fps for sound movies when you want the best sound quality, although this is also sometimes used in silent work when improved picture quality is required.

Another facility often fitted to more expensive projectors is a single frame projection device, the idea being that you can stop the film at any

Kodak Ektasound projector

A top class sound projector – Eumig 820 Sonomatic

single frame and examine that frame closely on the screen. Because of the amount of heat produced by the projection lamp and the delicate nature of the material from which the film is made, a heat filter is generally positioned automatically between the projection lamp and the film when the single frame button is pressed.

Movie projectors achieved a major step forward a few years ago when automatic threading was introduced; these days practically all amateur movie projectors are self-threading. You simply insert the end of the film into a slot, switch the projector on, and the projector threads itself correctly, automatically aligning the film in the projection gate. Anyone who has threaded an 8mm cine projector manually will know what a blessing this automatic threading is.

Screens

A great many amateur home movie makers completely ruin their movies by not projecting them on to a proper screen. Instead they use a sheet pinned to the wall, a white-painted wall itself, or even (believe me, I have seen it!) a wall painted a light colour – cream, pink, blue or green.

For the sake of the relatively low cost of a proper screen it is simply not worth while using anything else. A properly designed screen is self-supporting, stretches tightly so that there are no wrinkles, and has a surface specially designed to give a clear, bright, sharp picture. For use in the home with Super 8 movies, a screen with its longest dimension 36 or 48 inches is more than adequate for most purposes. If you try to project to a size larger than this the shortcomings of the very small picture size will quickly become obvious.

The material from which your screen is made has a marked effect on the brightness and quality of the picture. The cheapest type of screen is simple matt white plastic which gives an evenly bright picture from whichever direction you look at it. But that brightness is rather on the low side. For this reason matt white screens are normally used only when the projector is particularly powerful or when the distance between the projector and the screen can be kept relatively short.

Screens coated with aluminium or other metallic paint are much brighter than the matt white type but one disadvantage is that the brightness falls off as you move towards the side of the screen, so to get the best effect the audience must be seated fairly centrally in front of the screen.

The most popular type of screen with the amateur is the glass beaded type and, as the name implies, the surface is coated with many millions of tiny glass beads which reflect the image projected on to them very efficiently. Like the metallised screen, the glass beaded type gives a very bright picture indeed from directly in front of it, but the brightness falls off sharply as you view it from the side. So the remarks I made about the metallised screen apply even more so to this glass beaded type. Another disadvantage that the glass beaded type has, in my opinion, is that the pattern of the glass beads can become obtrusive if you view the screen from too close a distance; the general appearance is rather like coarse grain on the film.

A similar problem occurs with the fourth type of screen, and the most expensive, the lenticular type. The surface of this type of screen has a metallic appearance and consists of minute vertical channels which reflect the image evenly to any position in front of it.

For use in the home, I personally prefer the matt white plastic type of screen. It seems to me to be perfectly bright enough for domestic use because the projector is seldom more than about eight feet from it and the picture is adequately bright enough. It is also free from the disturbing patterns given by the glass beaded and lenticular type of screens and has the advantage that it can be viewed with equal ease from virtually any position. And, of course, it is also the least expensive.

Setting up the Projector

When you are going to have a film show, whether it be simply for the family and friends or if you are giving a film show at a public meeting, for example, always make sure that you have the projector set up, the film threaded, the screen erected, and everything else ready before the audience arrives and sits down. Nothing annoys an audience more than someone rushing about with bits of cable and film reels, setting up screens, and generally getting in everyone's way – it gets the evening off to a bad start.

If the show is to take place in your own living room, position the screen where everyone can see it easily without having to sit in an awkward position and with the screen at a sensible height from the ground.

Personally, I find that the easiest thing to do is simply set up the screen in front of the television set because in my living room, as in most other people's, the seating tends to be arranged for easy viewing of the television set (which must, I suppose, say something for modern standards of living).

Even more important than the height of the screen is the height of the projector relative to the screen. The lens should be at the same height as the centre of the screen in order to produce a perfectly rectangular picture. If you have the projector at a lower level than the centre of the screen, you have to tilt the projector up slightly so that the picture fits on to the screen properly. This produces a wedge shaped picture, narrower at the bottom than at the top, and not uniformly sharp. The reason for this is that because the projector is tilted up the distance from the projector lens to the screen is shorter at the bottom of the picture than it is at the top and the top of the picture therefore receives effectively more enlargement than the bottom, giving rise to the wedge shape. And because projection lenses are usually fairly wide aperture, the depth of field is relatively shallow and it becomes quite impossible to have the whole of the picture in focus at any one time. The best way to position the projector correctly is on a proper projector stand, but if you do not have one of these put it on a pile of books on top of an ordinary table.

Another important point to remember when you set your projector up ready for a show is to give the gate a good clean with a soft brush to remove any hairs or bits of emulsion from previous films that may otherwise accumulate there. This will ensure that your films are free from specks, hairs and the like when you project them and will give the whole show a much more professional appearance.

It is worth keeping your splicer and a supply of splicing tapes near the projector as well. Films do not often break during projection, but you can be quite sure that if one does it will be when you are showing films to an audience you particularly want to impress. So impress them with your dexterity in repairing the film instead!

And, of course, the one other piece of equipment that is an absolute must for any movie show is a spare projector lamp. Again, by the law of averages or any other law for that matter, projection lamps always burn out at the least convenient time.

If you have several reels of film to show, your audience will thank you to get on with showing them rather than rewinding each reel at the end of showing it. As long as you have a spare reel of the maximum size that your projector will take you will run into no problems during the showing and you can then rewind all the films the following morning when you are on your own.

The Show Itself

The fundamental and basic rule of putting on a home movie show is not to show too much. A total of an hour's viewing of home movies is enough for any audience, and the maximum length for any one film should be no more than twenty minutes.

If you have one major film to show, perhaps a twenty minute movie of your holidays, which you will have carefully edited to the correct length, it often improves the show if you can start with two or three short pieces. A good way round this is to use commercially-produced cartoons and other short films as your 'fillers'. The movie-making magazines nearly always carry advertisements offering these short commercially-produced films for sale and in most large towns there is a film library where you can hire films just as you borrow books from a normal library.

As to the selection of these fillers, try to choose something which will not be too much like the main movie you are going to show. For example, if you are going to show a twenty minute movie of your holiday, avoid travelogue type films. Cartoons are always popular with everyone from two-year olds upwards, and you can often find well-filmed natural history movies in most film libraries; these, too, have an almost universal appeal.

Set out all the reels of film on the projection table before you start so that you do not have to fumble about looking for the correct one at any point in the programme.

Sound for Accompaniment

Even if your movie camera is not a sound model there is nothing to stop you adding separate sound as background to your film, if you have a tape recorder. Obviously you cannot produce a sound track that is synchronised perfectly with the film, but you can record background music and a commentary or voice-over, as it is known in professional circles. In fact, you do not even need a tape recorder; you can use a record player, but this can lead to a bit of dashing about between the record player controls and those of the projector, so a tape recorder is a better idea if you have one.

There are a great many records and tapes available with suitable background music for all types of movies. Many of these records are specially produced for home movie makers and you do not need to apply for (or pay for) the right to transfer the music for use as a sound track on your films; with ordinary records and tapes, of course, you must do this otherwise you are contravening the copyright law.

When you have gained a little experience in adding sound as background to your movies you will find that the tape recorder can be used in much the same way as a film editing set-up to enable you to fit the appropriate music to any sequence in your movie.

When you play back the music along with your film, try to position an extension speaker from the tape recorder alongside the screen so that the sound and the pictures are reaching you from the same direction; it can be quite confusing to an audience to have the music coming from behind them when they are looking at pictures in front of them. And do not have the music too loud, especially if you are giving a commentary about the film separately as opposed to pre-recorded. In fact, if you are giving your commentary while the film is running, it is as well to position the tape recorder near the projector so that you can turn down the volume of the background music while you are speaking and turn it up again when it is required simply as background.

Sound striping

I mentioned in the chapter on sound movies that there is a system for adding sound to ordinary silent Super 8 movies. This is called sound striping and it can be used as long as you have a projector which enables sound recording to take place – such as the Ektasound projector I mentioned in the last chapter. There are several companies which offer a sound striping service; it consists of merely coating a narrow magnetic sound stripe, rather like recording tape, down the side of the processed film. You record your sound track on to this while the film is running through the special projector. It overcomes the problem of synchronising background music tape and films at the start of each performance, but it is still virtually impossible to achieve the perfect synchronisation that is needed for dialogue on a film.

APPENDIX 1 Depth of field tables

1. TYPICAL WIDE ANGLE LENS—7.5mm FOCAL LENGTH

LENS SETTING (feet)	DEPTH OF FIELD (FEET) AT f/1·4	f/2	f/2·8	f/4	f/5·6	f/8	f/11	f/16
∞	8½–∞	6¼–∞	4½–∞	3¼–∞	2½–∞	1¾–∞	1½–∞	1–∞
50	7½–∞	5½–∞	4¼–∞	3–∞	2¼–∞	1¾–∞	1½–∞	1–∞
15	5¾–∞	4¾–∞	3¾–∞	2¾–∞	2¼–∞	1¾–∞	1¼–∞	1–∞
10	5–∞	4–∞	3¼–∞	2¾–∞	2–∞	1¾–∞	1¼–∞	1–∞
7	4¼–24½	3½–∞	3–∞	2½–∞	2–∞	1½–∞	1¼–∞	1–∞
5	3½–9¼	3–15¼	2¾–114	2¼–∞	2–∞	1½–∞	1¼–∞	1–∞
4	3–6	2¾–8	2½–13¼	2¼–∞	2–∞	1½–∞	1¼–∞	1–∞

2. TYPICAL NORMAL LENS—15mm FOCAL LENGTH

LENS SETTING (feet)	f/1·4	f/2	f/2·8	f/4	f/5·6	f/8	f/11	f/16
∞	35½–∞	25–∞	17¾–∞	12½–∞	9–∞	6¼–∞	4½–∞	3¼–∞
50	21–∞	17–∞	13½–∞	10¼–∞	7¾–∞	5¾–∞	4¼–∞	3–∞
15	10¾–24½	9¾–33½	8½–66¾	7¼–∞	6–∞	4¾–∞	3¾–∞	2¾–∞
10	8–13¼	7½–5¼	6¾–19¾	6–33¾	5–11¾	4¼–∞	3½–∞	2¾–∞
7	6–8¼	5¾–9	5¼–10¼	4¾–13	4¼–19¾	3¾–94¾	3–∞	2½–∞
5	4½–5½	4¼–6	4¼–6¼	3¾–7¼	3½–8¾	3–12½	2¾–29¼	2¼–∞
4	3¾–4¼	3½–4½	3½–4¾	3¼–5¼	3–5¾	2¾–7¼	2½–10¼	2–∞

3. TYPICAL TELEPHOTO LENS—30mm FOCAL LENGTH

LENS SETTING (feet)	f/1·4	f/2	f/2·8	f/4	f/5·6	f/8	f/11	f/16
∞	142¼–∞	99½–∞	71–∞	49¼–∞	35¼–∞	24¾–∞	17¾–∞	12¼–∞
50	37½–75¾	33½–97¼	29¾–155¾	25¼–159	21–∞	16¾–∞	13½–∞	10–∞
15	13¾–16½	13¼–17¼	12½–18½	11¾–20½	10¾–24¼	9¾–32¾	8½–57½	7–∞
10	9½–10¾	9¼–11	9–11½	8½–12	8–13¼	7¼–15¼	6¾–18¾	5¾–31
7	6¾–7¼	6¼–7½	6½–7½	6¼–8	6–8¼	5¾–9	5¼–10	4¾–12½
5	4¾–5¼	4¾–5¼	4¾–5¼	4¾–5¼	4½–5½	4¼–5¾	4–6¼	3¾–7
4	3⅞–4⅛	3⅞–4⅛	3¾–4¼	3¾–4¼	3¾–4¼	3½–4½	3½–4¾	3¼–5

APPENDIX 2 Close up distances and areas (fixed focus lenses)

LENS FOCAL LENGTH (mm)	+1 DIOPTRE (Distance 31½in)		+2 DIOPTRE (Distance 17½in)		+3 DIOPTRE (Distance 12⅛in)	
	Width (in)	Height (in)	Width (in)	Height (in)	Width (in)	Height (in)
9	18½	14	10¼	7¾	7⅛	5⅜
13	12⅞	9⅝	7⅛	5⅜	4⅞	3¾
14	11¾	9	6½	5	4½	3½

Close up distances and areas (focusing lenses, set at infinity)

LENS FOCAL LENGTH (mm)	+1 DIOPTRE (Distance 39in)		+2 DIOPTRE (Distance 20in)		+3 DIOPTRE (Distance 13in)	
9	25	18½	12½	9¼	8¼	6
12·5	18	13¼	9	6½	6	4½
15	15	11	7½	5½	5	3¾
20	11¼	8¼	5½	4	3¾	2¾
27	8¼	6	4	3	2¾	2
32	6¾	5	3½	2½	2¼	1¾
36	6¼	4½	3	2¼	2	1½
40	5½	4	2¾	2	2	1¼
48	4¾	3½	2½	1¾	1½	1

APPENDIX 3 Projection chart

LENS FOCAL LENGTH (mm)	PICTURE SIZE AT					
	8ft	10ft	15ft	20ft	25ft	30ft
15	25 × 34	32 × 42	48 × 64	64 × 85	80 × 107	96 × 128
20	19 × 25	24 × 32	36 × 48	48 × 64	60 × 80	72 × 96
25	15 × 20	19 × 25	29 × 38	38 × 51	48 × 64	58 × 77
35		13 × 18	20 × 27	27 × 36	34 × 45	41 × 55

All picture sizes in inches

APPENDIX 4 Film running times

LENGTH (Feet)	18 FPS Min	Sec	24 FPS Min	Sec
50	3	20	2	30
100	6	40	5	
150	10		7	30
200	13	20	10	
250	16	40	12	30
300	20		15	
350	23	20	17	30
400	26	40	20	

APPENDIX 5 Super 8 colour films

MAKE	FILM	SPEED (ASA) Daylight	Tungsten	PROCESS PAID	REMARKS
Agfa	Super 8	25	40	Yes	
	Super 8 Sound	25	40	Yes	For sound cameras only
Boots	Colourcine	25	40	Yes	
Dixons	Prinzcolor	25	40	Yes	
GAF	Color Movie Type A	25	40	Yes	
Kodak	Kodachrome 40 Type A	25	40	Yes	
	Kodachrome 40 Type A Sound	25	40	Yes	For sound cameras only
	Ektachrome 40	25	40	No	
	Ektachrome 160	100	160	No	
	Ektachrome 160 Sound	100	160	No	For sound cameras only
	Ektachrome 160 Type G	160	160	No	Universal material for all types of lighting without using filter.
3M	Color Movie	25	40	Yes	

Appendix 6 When things go wrong

No matter how careful you are when you are making your movies there are, inevitably, times when something goes wrong, and the results are disappointing. So to help you avoid making the same mistake twice, here is a list of typical faults, their causes, and how to prevent them happening again.

1 Picture unsharp

Cause:
(a) With fixed focus cameras you were too close to your subject.
(b) With variable focus cameras you had not set the focusing control to the correct distance for your subject.
Remedy:
Focus very carefully, especially when using a telephoto lens or a zoom lens at its maximum telephoto setting.

2 Blurred or jumping pictures

Cause:
(a) You have loaded your cine camera or projector incorrectly; you can check which by carefully re-loading your projector. If the problem persists your camera was incorrectly loaded.
(b) Your camera has a fault.
(c) Your projector may need adjusting or the film may need cleaning.
Remedy:
(a) Follow the loading instructions for your camera and projector.
(b) Have your camera checked over by a qualified repair mechanic.
(c) Have your projector checked over. Clean the film with a proper movie film cleaner.

3 Pictures too light

Cause:
(a) You have partly covered the meter window with your finger.
(b) The batteries in your camera may be nearly exhausted or not making proper contact.

(c) The subject was predominantly dark.

Remedy:

(a) Be careful not to place your fingers where they can obscure the meter window.

(b) Replace the batteries in your camera or, if they are new, clean the contacts with a coarse cloth.

(c) If your camera has an exposure over-ride control, set it to $-\frac{1}{2}$ or -1 stop for dark subjects.

4 Pictures too dark

Cause:

(a) You have tried to film in conditions which were too dark for the film in your camera.

(b) The subject was predominantly light.

Remedy:

(a) If the under-exposure warning device appears in your viewfinder, do not shoot the sequence, or put a higher speed film in the camera.

(b) If your camera has an exposure over-ride control, set it to $+\frac{1}{2}$ or $+1$ stop for light subjects.

5 Pictures misty or lacking in contrast

Cause:

Your lens (or auxiliary filter if you are using one) was dirty.

Remedy:

Clean the lens or filter with special lens cleaning tissue, NOT a handkerchief.

6 Black, fuzzy areas in pictures

Cause:

Your fingers or the camera strap were in front of the camera lens. These areas could also be light in tone if they were in sunlight.

Remedy:

Make sure that the lens is unobstructed. If your camera is a reflex type you will be able to see this through the viewfinder.

7 Black spots in the picture

Cause:
Specks of dust or grit in the gate of the camera or projector. If the spots remain stationary relative to the picture when you adjust the projector framing control, the trouble is in the camera, but if they move with the picture the dirt is in the projector.
Remedy:
Clean your camera and projector before you put each film through.

8 Vertical scratches on the film

Cause:
Grit in the camera or projector which scratches the film as it passes.
Remedy:
Keep your camera and projector clean.

9 Overall foggy green pictures

Cause:
Your film was either outdated or had been stored in hot, humid conditions.
Remedy:
Always use fresh film and store it in cool, dry conditions (preferably in a fridge) before use. And when the film has been exposed, have it processed promptly.

When you are carrying film in a car, do not leave it in a closed glove compartment or in direct sunlight because it can quickly become overheated.

10 Overall bluish pictures

Cause:
You have used your film in daylight without using the conversion filter.
Remedy:
If your camera has a filter switch, make sure it is in the correct position for the type of lighting.

11 Streaks or spots of light

Cause:
Flare as a result of direct sunlight falling on the camera lens.
Remedy:
Take care to avoid direct light falling on the lens.

12 Film completely black

Cause:
The film has been completely unexposed.
Remedy:
Check that the film is correctly loaded and that the lens is not covered. When Super 8 film has been exposed, the word 'EXPOSED' appears on the piece of film in the cartridge aperture.

Check also that the meter is operating. Change the batteries if necessary, or clean the battery and camera contacts with a coarse cloth.

Further reading

How to Edit by H. Baddeley, (Focal Press)
Home Movies Made Easy Eastman Kodak Co (Eastman Kodak)
The Super 8 Film Maker's Handbook by A. Myron Matzkin, (Focal Press)
Super 8mm Movie Making Simplified by A. Myron Matzkin, (Amphoto)
How to Title by L. F. Minter, (Focal Press)
All-in-one Cine Book by Paul Petzold, (Focal Press)
How to make Colour Films by C. L. Thomson, (Focal Press)
How to Plan your Super 8 Movies by C. V. Willson, (Focal Press)

Acknowledgements

With the following exceptions the illustrations in this book are copyright of the author.

Pages 12, 95, 99, 110 (top) courtesy of Kodak Ltd; pages 13, 83, 104 courtesy of Photopia International Group; pages 14, 108, 110 (bottom) courtesy of Eumig (UK) Ltd; page 32 courtesy of Photax Ltd; page 65 courtesy of Paterson Products Ltd; pages 97, 105 courtesy of CZ Scientific Instruments Ltd.

Index

Entries in italics indicate illustrations.

David & Charles have a book on it

Making Wildlife Movies: An Introduction by Christopher Parsons. This book tells the beginner how to film wild creatures successfully and satisfyingly. The author shows how to plan a film, outlines basic rules, and describes tips and short cuts which will save time and money. He also gives clear instructions on how to make simple accessories at home.

Advice on filming animals, birds, fish and insects is included, with invaluable information on more technical aspects, such as build-up sequences, editing and sound, that are well within the ability of most of us, once we know how to approach them. Illustrated.

Practical Photographic Enlarging by Derek Watkins. For the true camera enthusiast making prints is probably the most satisfying of all stages of photography – the point at which all his earlier efforts at last bear fruit. This practical and well-illustrated book shows the keen amateur how to perfect his print quality and how to experiment with new materials to produce unusual and exciting results. It is written in a straightforward manner enabling the beginner as well as the advanced worker to gain valuable insights into this fascinating spare-time interest. Illustrated.

SLR Photography: A Handbook of the Single Lens Reflex by Derek Watkins. Get more out of your single lens reflex camera with this easy to follow guide presented in three stages. Part one deals with equipment – cameras, lenses and filters; part two covers picture making; part three deals with techniques – exposure meters, choice of films, colour and printing. 53 illustrations.

Good Photography Made Easy by Derek Watkins. This book helps everyone or get better results from their cameras, whether in holiday snapshots or in more ambitious photography. Whether you want to take good pictures in colour or black and white, with or without flash, the author shows simple, straightforward ways of getting the best results while saving money – not just in buying cameras, films and equipment, but by developing and printing your own pictures. Illustrated.

A Roadside Camera 1895–1915 by Michael E. Ware. 1895 was the first true year of the motor car in Britain and with it began the transformation of the roadside from a pedestrian, pedal and equestrian precinct into a highway monopolised by the internal combustion engine. Bicycles and horsedrawn traffic were still very much in evidence during the early years as was steam. Motor sports, fashions in cars and clothing and above all a new mobility for the family enable a very dramatic story to be told in pictures. *A . . . Camera series*. Illustrated.

A Country Camera 1844–1914 by Gordon Winter. One of the most popular books we have had the privilege to publish, this is an enthralling photographic record of what life in the countryside was like in the years from the beginning of photography to the end of the Golden Age in August 1914. The result is a piece of social history, and a portrait of a now-vanished world. Illustrated.

A Canalside Camera 1845–1930 by Michael E. Ware. The years between 1845 and 1930 saw the heyday of the British canal system. Early canal photographs are rare; photography had not been invented when the first canals were built and the new medium was seldom used to record industry and transport. Much painstaking research has gone into this remarkable collection of prints; *A Canalside Camera* records canal construction, operation and maintenance, craft and cargoes, and the people involved, at work and at leisure. *A . . . Camera series*. Illustrated throughout.

Early Wildlife Photographers by C. A. W. Guggisberg with a foreword by Eric Hosking, Hon FRPS, FIIP. When did wildlife enthusiasts first drop the gun for the camera? Professional zoologist C. A. W. Guggisberg presents the story of the dedicated early nature photographers from Cherry and Richard Kearton, Schilling, Bengt Berg and Seaton Gordon to Frank Chapman. 100 illustrations.